WORLD WAR I

An AP Centennial Commemorative Edition

The Associated Press

Edited by
Raf Casert and Virginia Mayo

The Associated Press
200 Liberty Street
New York, NY 10281
www.ap.org

No part of this publication may be re-produced, distributed or transmitted in any form or by any means, without prior written permission. This is a work of nonfiction adapted from articles and content by journalists of The Associated Press and published with permission.

Copyright © 2018 by The Associated Press

All photos courtesy of The Associated Press unless indicated otherwise.

Project Management by Peter Costanzo
Design and Production by BNGO Books
Cover Design by Chuck Zoeller
Visit AP Books: www.ap.org/books
All photographs provided by AP Images: www.apimages.com

Frontispiece photo: The U.S. 42nd Division monument at Fere-en-Tardenois France, Saturday, May 26, 2018. The memorial, a bronze sculpted by British artist James Butler, represents an American soldier carrying the body of his dead comrade. Memorial Day commemorations will take place in the Aisne-Marne district as well as other areas to remember the fallen and those who have served. (AP Photo/Virginia Mayo)

*Dedicated to all AP journalists
who have lost their lives covering war.*

FOREWORD

IT WAS SUPPOSED TO BE the "War to End All Wars," a great clash of nations that began with stirring words of duty and patriotism and ended with 14 million dead, empires destroyed and the social order torn asunder. Instead of securing peace and justice, World War One fomented revolutions and counter-revolutions across the world, paving the way for the tyranny of Hitler and Stalin and an even greater global slaughter, World War Two, a generation later. With most combatants exhausted and traumatized by years of bloodshed, the clearest winner was the United States, which did not enter the war until the final two years and emerged as the world's economic powerhouse. Nevertheless, nearly 117,000 American service members died, albeit a fraction of the Germans, French, Russians and Britons who perished.

Through the prism of history, World War One stands as perhaps the ultimate "War of Choice," a conflict that could have been avoided through skilled diplomacy and better judgment. What began as an attempt by the Austro-Hungarian Empire to punish Serbia for its suspected involvement in the assassination of the heir to the Imperial throne spiraled into a continental then global war as a complicated alliance system pulled the other major combatants into the slaughter. The family that held the Austro-Hungarian throne had ruled different parts of Europe for nearly nine centuries. Its reign ended with defeat in World War One.

Almost all of the men and women who experienced World War One—in the trenches of France and Flanders, or the deserts of Arabia or the fields and factories of the home front—are gone. With them the world risks losing many of the lessons of that war and an appreciation of the pain and sacrifice endured by those who lived it. On the centennial of the end of World War One, The Associated Press has collected a series of stories tracing the arc of the conflict, from Sarajevo where the Austrian heir was slain through the agony of trench warfare and America's entry, which turned the tide against Germany and its allies.

In some of the reports, we can gain insights into the war and its warriors. There was the idealistic young American Alan Seeger who volunteered to fight for France and its motto of "Liberty, Fraternity and Equality." He was killed in action before his country even entered the war, leaving behind the haunting, prophetic poem "I Have A Rendezvous With Death," President John F. Kennedy's favorite. We can sense the lifelong suffering of Turkish soldier Mehmet Emin Eroz through the recollections of his son Kenan. His father, like many combat veterans, did not talk much about the war. Instead, "we could see the ugly side of war on my father's body. His feet were full of wounds." We can see what motivated an American president, Woodrow Wilson, to enter the war after promising the American people that he never would.

—Robert H. Reid, Senior Managing Editor, Stars & Stripes

CONTENTS

Foreword	vii
The Tragedy of World War I in One Soldier's Story	1
Sarajevo: The Political Slaying that Set off World War I	8
Blind to Tragedy, Europe Started World War I	11
World War I Trenches in England Highlight Training for the Real Horrors of War	14
Tour De France, Too, Was Steeped in World War I Horrors	17
Before 'Saving Private Ryan,' Pvt. Smith Was Saved	21
World War I Spread Flowers Around Too, and Not Only Poppies	26
Cultural Heritage So Often One of First Victims of War	29
World War I Aviation Still Alive, and Swooping, at Aerodrome in New York	32
World War I: The Horrors of War that Inspired Innovative Art	35
The Day France Relied on Its Cabbies to Boost Its War Effort	40
They Never Wilted. Poppies Live on as Enduring Symbol of the War	43
In 1914 Amid the Great War, the Greatest of Champagne Vintages	46
WORLD WAR I: A REMEMBRANCE IN PICTURES	49
A Century Later, British Army Honors Soldiers Killed in WWI	56
Christmas 1914: The Day Even World War I Showed Humanity	59
A Landscape Shaped By War	63
A Century Later, a Mythic Thud of a Football in Wartime Is Still Heard	65
First Gas Attacks Unleashed New Horrors and Changed Warfare	68

World War I

Victor in the Boston Marathon One Year, a Victim of World War I the Next	72
Memories Still Haunt Both Sides of the Gallipoli Tragedy	75
Alan Seeger, Poet-Soldier, Who Fought as an American with France in World War I	78
The United States Joined World War I to Make the Difference	82
Innovations a Century Ago, but Still with Us	87
Vimy—The World War I Battle that Defined Canada	92
Spy, Temptress, Victim? Mata Hari Still Eludes Definition	94
One Victorous Battle that Became a Defining Moment for the United States	98
World War I Munitions Still Making Their Way Onto the Beaches an Ocean Away	102
One Lone Submarine Brought World War I Home to the United States	105
Death in the Final Minutes of World War I Highlighted Folly of War	108
AP Was There	111
Afterword	114
WORLD WAR I: TIMELINE OF EVENTS	118
WORLD WAR I: PHOTO TIMELINE	124
About the Editors and Contributors	175
Bylines	176
Acknowledgments	180

THE TRAGEDY OF WORLD WAR I IN ONE SOLDIER'S STORY

Nieuwkerke, Belgium

IN A NEATLY CLIPPED CORNER of the Westhof Farm Cemetery, an Australian family huddled around the grave of Pvt. Andrew Bayne. One century after World War I, the family found closure in homage to a forebear who had traveled half the world to meet his death, his stomach ripped open by an exploding shell, in the horrors of Flanders Fields.

Bayne left his wife, Katie, with four young children in Brisbane and a prescient letter of regret: "What a dammed fool I was to ever have enlisted."

Bayne's remains lie alongside other Commonwealth victims and a handful of German dead, the rows of pristine white tombstones stretching over rich, undulating pastures. Belgium and France are still scarred by over 1,000 graveyards, countless bomb craters, rusting gas shells, bunkers and trenches that tore apart the Western Front for four years.

World War I

The front line of death and destruction burned through the Alps, Central Europe, the Balkans and Russia, spilling into present-day Turkey and reaching beyond to the Middle East and as far as China. It claimed some 14 million lives—5 million civilians and 9 million soldiers, sailors and airmen from 28 countries, from India to South Africa to the United States. The 1914-18 conflict was so unprecedented in its scope and savagery that it became known simply as "The Great War." At least 7 million troops were left permanently disabled and families across the globe, much like Bayne's, were wrecked.

Despite the vows of "never again" across a shell-shocked world, the outcome of the conflict only sowed the bitter seeds that led to World War II and more slaughter. And the nationalist tensions that set off the killing never really died.

For Kaylene Biggs, misty-eyed after finally facing the grave of her great-grandfather in the small cemetery, the war's far-reaching legacy makes remembrance all the more important. "It isn't until you do visit the battlefields that you realize the huge amount of loss and sacrifice."

"Now, it seems so peaceful," she said amid the twitter of birds and the faraway galloping of a horse.

The early summer of 1914 seemed just as tranquil to most Europeans. By that time, the Bayne family had already been in Australia for two years, hoping to build a richer life after toiling for meager rewards on a Scottish farm.

Little did they know that Europe would not let them go so easily.

SUDDENLY, SARAJEVO

The Ottoman and Austro-Hungarian empires had often clashed over borders in the restive Balkans, but somehow diplomats had muddled through without plunging the world into war. Little prepared Europe for June 28, 1914, when a gunshot from Serb nationalist Gavrilo Princip killed Austro-Hungarian Crown Prince Franz Ferdinand in Sarajevo.

So shocking was the murder, so constricting its consequences, that no diplomacy could stop the slow wheels of intricate alliances and oblique agreements that pulled the continent into full war by Aug. 4.

Adding to the combustible mix was the perception among several great powers that Germany was bent on military expansion to boost its standing as second to none in Europe. An arms race had been building for several years. In Berlin, there was an almost claustrophobic feeling of encirclement.

"You get something in 1914 like a perfect storm," said historian Margaret MacMillan, of Oxford University. "So in those five weeks, Europe, instead of pulling back from the brink, puts itself toward the brink. And the results are catastrophic. And you look at it, and you think, 'You don't have to be doing this.'"

When the pieces of the puzzle finally fell into place that August, the Entente Powers including Britain, France and Russia faced the Central Powers of the German and Austro-Hungarian empires.

Germany opened the Western Front with a massive attack through Luxembourg and Belgium, hoping to knock out France before Russia had a chance to mobilize in the east. It was hoping to count victory in weeks, not years. But Belgium was tougher to get through than expected, and French and British troops stopped the German onslaught at the Marne River northeast of Paris.

"At the beginning, people thought it was a war worth fighting," MacMillan said. "They all had good reason to fight. They didn't, most of them, foresee what the war would turn into."

The war quickly became a deadly stalemate the likes of which had never been seen. Over the next years, each side attempted a series of massive offensives that failed to break the deadlock but caused horrific carnage—up to 1 million dead in the French Battle of the Somme alone. The Gallipoli campaign in Turkey was so ghastly it turned into a seminal event for Australian and New Zealand nationhood.

Sometimes tens of thousands would die in a single day, Germans and Austro-Hungarians as swiftly as British and French. Artillery was relentless. Toxic gas was introduced in modern warfare with devastating effect. The poison wafted across trenches, killing and maiming whoever took a breath. Because of it, the need for fresh manpower was enormous—and the reach of the British Empire was global. One million Indian troops alone served overseas under British command. A New Zealand memorial in Flanders simply says "From the uttermost ends of the earth."

World War I

It was only a matter of time before the war turned up at Andrew Bayne's doorstep in Brisbane.

"THEY HAVE GOT ME"

Bayne was hardly gung-ho about the war. What turned things around, Biggs said, was that "one day in the street, he was handed a white feather," at the time a universal sign for cowardice. "So he went and joined up." His dreams of setting up a farm were replaced with the horrors of Europe: the trenches, the mud, the gas, the booming artillery.

He enlisted in June 1916, left Australia four months later—and arrived in France from England in March of the following year, just one indication of the pace of war a century ago.

Bayne was not the only family member to go. In a sign of how global the war could be, his brother John enlisted in the Australian Light Horse, fought on Gallipoli in Turkey and in Beersheba in current-day Israel. Another brother, Adam, joined the Canadian forces and went to fight in France; a third, Bill, fought with the British. They all survived.

Family archives showed that Andrew Bayne fought at Bullecourt in northern France, where two battles cost Australia 10,000 casualties and hardly moved the front line. Bullecourt villagers coming back said there was no way of knowing where their houses had once been. Such devastation was par for the course during the years of stalemate.

Bayne, like so many millions of soldiers, long remained hopeful as the war stretched into its fourth year. The Germans, he wrote home, "are about starved out and they can't last much longer." He added, "Cheer up. I will be with you yet."

On Aug. 19, 1917, a German shell burst close to him as he was on the Ypres front holding the line close to Messines Ridge, little more than a molehill but a killer of thousands on both sides. The pain and agony were recorded matter-of-factly in a witness report: "The wounds were left arm, right of face and stomach—the latter a bad one."

Bayne could still call for a stretcher and, before losing consciousness, uttered: "They have got me." He died soon afterward at age 32.

Had he held out longer, he might have benefited by the U.S. entry into the war.

"EUROPE'S WAR," AMERICA'S BREAKTHROUGH

For most Americans, it began as "Europe's war." Many German, Scandinavian and Irish immigrants saw no reason to help the British and pacifism was all the rage in a country still traumatized by its own Civil War. A 1915 hit song in America carried the name: "I Didn't Raise My Boy To Be A Soldier."

But Germany's policy of unrestricted submarine attacks undermined neutrality. In 1915, a German submarine sank the British liner Lusitania, killing 128 Americans. President Woodrow Wilson responded that America was "too proud to fight" but demanded Germany halt attacks on passenger ships. Even modest steps to build up the U.S. Navy and an Army Reserve met strong public opposition.

Three things tipped the scales: somewhat overdramatized reports of German atrocities in Belgium and elsewhere; Germany's decision in January 1917 to resume unrestricted submarine warfare; and a clumsy, ill-timed overture by the Germans to Mexico.

On April 2, 1917, President Wilson asked Congress to declare war on Germany to make the world "safe for democracy." U.S. troops did not arrive in strength in Europe until the following year.

They found themselves in the middle of the end game.

Russian Czar Nicholas II was forced out and the new Bolshevik government under Vladimir Lenin signed a peace treaty on March 3, 1918, allowing Germany to center all of its remaining energy on the Western Front. Germans advanced to the point of bringing Paris into artillery range but allied counterattacks and the arrival of up to 2.1 million American soldiers tipped the balance for good.

"They were essential in turning the tide," said Belgian military historian Luc De Vos of Leuven University. "There was a real deadlock in the war" and the other combatants were exhausted, he said. "The 2 million Americans—young, enthusiastic troops—they attacked and they were everywhere on the front."

More than 116,500 American service members were killed and some U.S. soldiers now lie buried in the huge swath of Flanders fields where Bayne was also laid to rest.

With German forces in retreat, a revolutionary government seized power in Berlin and stopped fighting on Nov. 11, 1918. The Versailles peace treaty sealed Germany's defeat the following June 28, five years to the day after the Sarajevo shooting set off the war.

SCAR TISSUE

The Great War left the United States at the dawn of what would become known as the American century. In Europe and beyond, the empires that launched the conflict—Germany, Austria-Hungary, the Ottomans and Russia—all collapsed. The war allowed Lenin to establish the Soviet Union. In Germany, defeat paved the way for the rise of Adolf Hitler.

At a personal level, the horrors of modern warfare and the massive loss of life produced the "Lost Generation," with millions left cynical, rootless and disillusioned by carnage and social upheaval. In literature, this generation included greats like Ernest Hemingway, T.S. Eliot and Erich Maria Remarque. It also affected millions of families around the world.

Bayne's wife Katie long refused to believe that he had died, since she apparently received a letter dated after his death. Biggs said her great grandmother went to meet every ship bringing soldiers home into Brisbane.

"My grandmother could remember one particular time being with her mother, chasing after a man who had just got off a returning warship, who she thought was Andrew," she said.

"They never had a funeral for him," Biggs added. "I cannot fathom the hurt."

For the rest of her life—over half a century—she would carry with her the last letter Andrew wrote, Biggs said.

Without Andrew, Katie Bayne struggled and scraped together money to take the children back to Scotland in 1920. Once there, life seemed even bleaker. She brought the family back to Australia three years later.

Amid the luxuries of the 21st century, her Australian descendants still consider remembrance a necessity.

THE LAST POST

Like the hundreds of thousands coming to Europe from across the world over the four years, the Baynes' pilgrimage has been multi-generational. Kaylene and her husband Peter also brought their three children.

The Tragedy of World War I in One Soldier's Story

"His children and his wife weren't able to come," said Kaylene's daughter Jaleesa, 18. "They, in a sense, didn't get closure but we are able to come here and to see what they always wanted to see."

From Gallipoli to Sarajevo to Verdun and Flanders Fields, countless memorials and cemeteries have stood in immaculate condition to take in crowds and host leaders from all sides for commemorations.

For Biggs and her family, a trip across the globe to a simple grave in a small cemetery has meant the world.

"With all this sadness, I am so thankful that he actually does have a grave, somewhere for his descendants to go to pay their respects," she said. "I feel comforted that his sacrifice has not been forgotten through time."

A few miles from Bayne's grave is Ypres, site of four war battles and home to the Menin Gate with its 54,000-plus names inscribed to the missing, never found in the fields of Flanders. Every evening at 8 p.m., the local fire brigade plays the Last Post in an eerily solemn tribute that has drawn big crowds throughout the centenary.

The contrast of peace and war amid the memorials and cemeteries could not be bigger for Jaleesa.

"You just cannot imagine that only 100 years ago, it was the middle of hell," she said. "You've seen the movies. You've read the books and stuff, but it is still incomprehensible.

"Now, it is a memorial to them. It is so peaceful."

SARAJEVO: THE POLITICAL SLAYING THAT SET OFF WORLD WAR I

Sarajevo, Bosnia-Herzegovina

A CENTURY AFTER GAVRILO PRINCIP ignited World War I with a shot from his handgun, the baby-faced Serb teenager who assassinated the Austro-Hungarian crown prince in Sarajevo in 1914 still provokes controversy.

His legacy has been molded time and again to meet political agendas in the Balkans, which remains a smoldering patchwork of ethnic and religious rivalries.

Nikola Princip crossed himself and stood silently recently in front of a Sarajevo chapel plaque that read "The Heroes of St. Vitus Day." The list starts with Gavrilo Princip's name for the assassination he carried out on that sacred Serb holiday of June 28.

Sarajevo: The Political Slaying that Set off World War I

"He lived and died for his ideas to liberate and unite the southern Slavs. May he rest in peace," the 81-year-old man said, lighting a candle.

A few blocks away, another plaque marks the spot where Princip killed Crown Prince Franz Ferdinand. There, Halida Basic, a 72 year-old Bosnian Muslim, has a different view.

"He was a killer, a terrorist. He did it because he wanted Bosnia to be part of Greater Serbia," she said.

Barely a month after the 19-year-old fired his shots, Europe, and eventually the world, was at war.

Austria accused Serbia of masterminding the assassination. Backed by Germany, Austria attacked Serbia, whose allies, Russia and France, were quickly drawn in. Britain, its sprawling Commonwealth empire, quickly, and the United States, eventually, also joined the fighting.

When the mass slaughter known as the Great War ended in 1918, it had claimed some 14 million lives—5 million civilians and 9 million soldiers, sailors and airmen—and left another 7 million troops permanently disabled.

For his part, Princip was immediately arrested and died in captivity months before the war ended.

When the centenary remembrance of the assassination approached in the Bosnian capital of Sarajevo in 2014, the old entrenched positions resurfaced.

"Gavrilo Princip will, just like the past 100 years, remain a hero for some and a terrorist to others," said the head of the Sarajevo History Institute, Husnija Kamberovic. "It is a matter of feelings toward what he did, and not a matter of serious historical arguments."

The split follows Bosnia's ethnic divisions.

Christian Orthodox Serbs celebrate Princip as someone who saw Bosnia as part of the Serb national territory. The same idea inspired the Serbs in 1992 to fight the decision by Muslim Bosnians and Catholic Croats to declare the former republic of Bosnia independent when Serb-dominated Yugoslavia fell apart.

In Serb history books, the "great liberation act" of Princip and his comrades is described for over 20 pages.

"They were heroes who were ready to sacrifice their own lives for freedom and liberation," said Jovan Medosevic, a primary school history teacher in the Bosnian Serb town of Pale, near Sarajevo.

That's exactly what makes Princip unpopular among Muslim Bosnians and Catholic Croats. In their official textbooks, Princip is mentioned in just one sentence as a member of a secret terrorist organization who "did not assassinate Franz Ferdinand to liberate Bosnia from the occupier, but wanted Bosnia to become a part of Kingdom of Serbia," high school student Ermin Lazovic said.

A century ago, Muslim Bosnians and Catholic Croats preferred to stay in the big Austrian empire that had brought progress, law and order. Serbia was already in the process of destroying all mosques on its territory after it had liberated itself from the Ottoman Empire.

For the Serbs, it is beyond doubt that Austria and Germany were the instigators of World War I, not Princip or the Serbs.

"We have no new facts and we can only reinterpret old documents," Bosnian Serb historian Draga Mastilovic said. "So are we now supposed to accept the Austro-Hungarian position that Serbia caused that war?"

He said he understood why Germans and Austrians want to promote their version of events. "It is not easy to carry the burden of having caused two world-wide bloodbaths in the 20th century," he said.

A Bosnian rock group has even written a song about the sunny morning in 1914 when, according to their lyrics, Princip became a "hero to some, a criminal to others, while probably his own soul is still wandering, somewhere in between."

Fixing the flower arrangement he laid in front of the little chapel in Sarajevo, Nikola Princip admitted he had a personal stake in the debate.

"Gavrilo Princip was my uncle," he said.

BLIND TO TRAGEDY, EUROPE STARTED WORLD WAR I

Saint-Symphorien, Belgium

BRITISH PVT. JOHN PARR SET OFF on his reconnaissance bike on the lookout for German troops amid the rolling farmland and woods south of Brussels in August 1914. It was the last anyone saw of 'Ole Man' Parr, the ironic nickname he won due to his tender age of 17. He became known as the first Commonwealth soldier to die on the Western Front of World War I, likely killed by German gunfire.

Another British private, George Ellison, was already moving to face the Germans in southern Belgium for the first battle of the two empires. He went on to survive the horrific slaughter of the Somme and Passchendaele and came back to the Belgian pastures, where he was shot and killed on Nov. 11, 1918—the last day of the war.

World War I

Now, Parr and Ellison lie separated by a few footsteps—and 9 million dead soldiers over four years—in the cemetery of Saint Symphorien. The jarring contrast of distance and death count symbolizes that, in the early August days of 1914, few knew what hell the great powers of the age unleashed when they declared war.

"They didn't, most of them, foresee what the war would turn into," said Oxford University historian Margaret MacMillan. "And if they had known what the war was going to be, four years of huge slaughter, consumption of resources, destruction in many cases of their own societies, they might have thought differently."

Nobody foresaw the cataclysm that would befall the world the day of Aug. 4, 1914, when the conflict erupted in full force with the German invasion of Belgium and the British declaration of war. Both sides believed the war would be over by Christmas. Instead, a battlefront scar would slowly and agonizingly rip across Europe, ravage whole societies and millions of families. It produced a moral wasteland in Germany that would become fertile ground for the rise of Nazism. Four empires would disappear.

One hundred years later, it has been a time for joint remembrance. In August 2014, French President Francois Hollande hosted his German counterpart Joachim Gauck near their common border in oft-disputed Alsace to underline their friendship despite bitterly fighting two world wars in the 20th century. Gauck also joined Britain's Prince William, his wife Catherine and brother Prince Harry at the Saint Symphorien cemetery for a similar remembrance.

It set off four years of centennial events from the United States to Russia, China to Australia, through Belgium, France, Germany and Britain—underscoring that there was hardly a place on the planet untouched by the calamity.

With soaring tensions over Ukraine and Russia, the causes of World War I have had special resonance in 2014. A century ago few thought war was imminent until the June 28 killing in Sarajevo of Archduke Franz Ferdinand of the Austro-Hungarian empire.

Yet those shots fired by Serb nationalist Gavrilo Princip in Bosnia-Herzegovina carried tragic echoes. A political puzzle of complicated alliances fell into place that inexorably closed in on total war between the alliance of German and the Austro-Hungarian empires and the Allied powers of Britain, France and Russia.

Then as now, global peace and prosperity did not seem an unreasonable expectation.

"Europe went so quickly from peace to war—five weeks, from the assassination June 28th in Sarajevo to a general war on Aug. 4," said MacMillan. "And you do feel, 'don't you realize what you will be throwing away.' People are on summer holidays in these lovely towns. Europe is getting more prosperous and they are about to throw themselves into this catastrophic struggle."

In a half dozen crises over the five years leading to the Great War, countries had always stepped back from the brink. This time though, "you had people who had decided for various reasons they were not going to back down."

Germany opened the Western Front on Aug. 4, sweeping into Belgium, hoping to overwhelm France before Russia had a chance to mobilize to the east.

The Schlieffen Plan was conceived as a lightning-fast operation that would bring German forces into Paris within weeks. It is why the fierce battles around Belgium's Liege and Mons have such significance—since holding up the Germans for a few days, even in defeat, delayed their operation and deprived them of a swift victory.

It is what gives the death of Parr—on Aug. 21, 1914—and some 1,500 British soldiers in Belgium military meaning, said Peter Francis of the Commonwealth War Graves Commission.

"It was an ordered defeat, if that makes sense," Francis said, "It is a defeat that bought time. It allowed the Schlieffen Plan to be held up and start to crumble. It was a defeat that bought another day."

Such defeats bought more than that. They bought another week, another month. And, in a sense, four more years.

WORLD WAR I TRENCHES IN ENGLAND HIGHLIGHT TRAINING FOR THE REAL HORRORS OF WAR

Gosport, England

TWO LINES OF TRENCHES FACE OFF across No Man's Land. A soldier marches, rifle in hand, along a ditch. These are instantly familiar images of World War I—but this is Britain, a century on and an English Channel away from the battlefields of the Western Front.

This overgrown and oddly corrugated patch of heathland on England's south coast was once a practice battlefield, complete with trenches, weapons and barbed wire. Thousands of troops trained here to take on the German army. After the 1918 victory—which cost 1 million Britons their lives—the site was forgotten, until it was recently rediscovered by a local official with an interest in military history.

World War I Trenches in England Highlight Training for the Real Horrors of War

Now the trenches are being used to reveal how the Great War transformed Britain—physically as well as socially. As living memories of the conflict fade, historians hope these physical traces can help preserve the story of the war for future generations.

"We've now lost our First World War veterans. You're not going to get a firsthand account," said Richard Osgood, an archaeologist with the Ministry of Defense, which owns the land. "In many ways, the truest witness is the archaeology and the legacy left behind."

The trenches, near the town of Gosport, about 80 miles (130 kilometers) south of London, were rediscovered a few months ago by Robert Harper, head of conservation at the local council. A military history buff, he noticed some crenellated lines on a 1950s aerial photograph of the area, and was startled to recognize the pattern of "the classic British trench system."

He was even more surprised when he had a look at the land—a local picnic spot—and found the contours of the trenches still clearly visible under a thick covering of bracken, gorse and grass. He could make out a front-line trench and several reserve rows, along with communications trenches and forward observation posts. And then there was an opposing set, 300 yards (meters) away.

"It was one of those jaw-dropping moments," Harper said.

"I've got five relatives buried on the Western Front. I think to myself, 'Did any of them train here?'"

Several other sets of practice trenches have been found in Britain, but this is easily the most extensive.

The discovery is already providing ammunition for those who reject the "lions led by donkeys" view of the war, which argues that incompetent officers led ill-prepared troops into needless slaughter.

Historian Dan Snow said the elaborate mock battlefield "shows how seriously they took the business of training."

"They had to send the guys out to France to do the hardest of tasks, something no one had done before, and that is defeat the German army when they were dug in," Snow said. "How to break that deadlock? Well, the answer is right here in front of us. Massive, massive preparation."

The find is being used to launch a campaign, Home Front Legacy, which aims to record as many physical traces of the war as possible. Even though the four-year conflict was largely fought outside Britain, the war transformed the country's landscape in ways that have often been forgotten.

It's hoped amateur historians will comb family archives, local newspapers and other sources for evidence of everything from military bases and prisoner-of-war camps to munitions factories, pillboxes and listening posts.

The project has the support of the defense ministry, which turns out to be keen on archaeology—perhaps unsurprisingly, since it owns 1 percent of Britain—and enlists volunteer soldiers to help with exploration on its lands.

Osgood said the aim at the mock battlefield is "to repopulate the landscape," to tell the stories of some of the troops who trained there. Soldiers from Britain, Canada, New Zealand and the U.S. all passed through this area, close to the major naval base of Portsmouth, on their way to the front.

It would only take the tiniest of objects, such as a lost cap badge, to provide a clue.

"These were real men in a real-life situation going out and sacrificing their lives," Harper said. "That emotional, human story—I'd love that to be the meat put on the bones of what we have."

TOUR DE FRANCE, TOO, WAS STEEPED IN WORLD WAR I HORRORS

Paris, France

BEFORE SUNRISE ON JUNE 28, 1914, a pack of cyclists set off from Paris on the 12th Tour de France. Hours later, an Austrian archduke stepped out in Sarajevo and was assassinated in the street, igniting the carnage of World War I.

One hundred years later, cycling's greatest race paid special tribute to the millions who fought and died in what came to be known as the Great War. Several stages of the famed Tour de France that year ran along the war's killing fields, trenches and fronts in northern France and Belgium.

The 1914 Tour was the last before a five-year suspension due to the war. Of the 145 riders that day, 15 of them, including three Tour champions, would die in the fighting.

World War I

In all, an estimated 45 cyclists who had raced in pre-war Tours were killed in the 1914-1918 war, according to cycling historian Jean-Paul Bourgier.

The Tour itself has a complicated history with the war. Its founder, Henri Desgrange, joined in the warmongering, using his L'Auto newspaper to issue a lusty call for his countrymen "to go get those bastards."

"When your rifle butt will be on their chest, they will ask you for forgiveness. Don't let them trick you. Pull the trigger without pity," Desgrange wrote, according to Graham Healy's book "The Shattered Peloton."

After the war, Desgrange pledged to never let a German rider compete in the Tour, a threat that was never carried out.

At the Tour in 2014, riders and fans had several occasions to pay homage to war victims: Stages 5 through 10 largely traced the 400-mile (645-kilometer) long Western Front, from Ypres, Belgium, to the Swiss border near the northeastern French city of Mulhouse.

An estimated 5 million combatants died on this front during the war, the British government estimates. Most are still buried there in immaculately landscaped military cemeteries or under farmers' fields in unmarked graves.

Stage 5 started in Ypres, the killing ground immortalized by Canadian soldier-poet John McCrae in his poem "In Flanders Fields:"

"We are the Dead. Short days ago
We lived, felt dawn, saw sunset glow,
Loved and were loved, and now we lie
In Flanders fields."

Riders assembled that day within sight of the Menin Gate, a memorial dedicated to the 54,405 British and Commonwealth casualties whose graves are not known.

Not far from the Stage 5 start was cycling's iconic Kemmelberg Hill. As recounted by Healy, Frenchman Camille Fily, at 17 the youngest-ever Tour rider, was shot and killed around there late in the war while serving as a bike messenger. Among the many nearby war memorials is the Kemmelberg French Ossuary, where the bodies of 5,294 French soldiers lie buried.

Tour De France, Too, Was Steeped in World War I Horrors

The Stage 6 start in Arras took riders near France's largest military cemetery, Notre-Dame-de-Lorette, where 40,058 French war dead are buried. Among them, most likely, is 1909 Tour champion Francois Faber of Luxembourg.

Less than a month after finishing ninth in the 1914 Tour, Faber enlisted in the French Foreign Legion. He was killed the following May during the Battle of Artois, just north of Arras. His body was never found, but a plaque in his memory can be seen in the Notre-Dame-de-Lorette church.

Faber won the 1909 Tour with a display of sheer dominance. He won 6 of its 14 stages, including five in a row—a record that still stands—and led the race from Stage 2 to the finish. He won despite breaking his chain a kilometer from the finish line in Paris. Carrying his bike, he ran to the finish line, where he was mobbed by fans.

Faber was offered a spot as his military unit's cyclist in 1915 but refused.

"I prefer to serve in the trenches. I know all about trench work and I have more chance of bringing down Germans there than as a cyclist," he said, according to Healy.

Stage 6 also took riders along Chemin des Dames, a 30-kilometer ridge road and the site of one of the most disastrous French offensives of the war, where hundreds of thousands of men were killed in only a few weeks.

Two other Tour champions died near the route of Stage 7, from the Champagne town of Epernay to the northeastern city of Nancy; Octave Lapize, the 1910 winner, and Lucien Petit-Breton, a two-time winner in 1907 and 1908.

Lapize, who once famously called Tour organizers "assassins" for sending riders up impossibly steep climbs in the Pyrenees mountains, died when his biplane was shot down in a dogfight on Bastille Day, 1917, near the village of Flirey. The Tour passed through Flirey in 2014.

Petit-Breton, who took part in nine of the first 12 Tours, was killed in an automobile accident while on an army mission near the front.

Stage 7 also passed Verdun, a pivotal World War I battlefield where an estimated 300,000 French and German troops were killed—most ripped apart by the apocalyptic shelling that permanently disfigured the landscape.

World War I

Before the riders left the battlefields behind and attacked the Alps, one last, poignant reminder of World War I awaited. As they traveled from Mulhouse to Besancon for the race's first rest day on July 15, the road passed close to the tiny village of Joncherey.

The village has a memorial to Jules-Andre Peugeot—a 21-year-old corporal killed in a skirmish with German troops on Aug. 2, 1914, making him the very first casualty on the war's Western Front.

BEFORE 'SAVING PRIVATE RYAN,' PVT. SMITH WAS SAVED

Barnard Castle, England

CARVED INTO THE SIMPLE OBELISK commemorating the fallen are the names of five sons of Margaret and John McDowell Smith. There's a story behind the name that isn't there—a sixth brother, Wilfred—and a century after World War I a local historian has dug out the details from archives.

Wilfred Smith's survival is a story of sacrifice amid a war that demanded so much of it from virtually every family in Britain.

Because long before there was the fictional tale of "Saving Private Ryan," there was the real-life story of saving Pvt. Smith.

The people of Barnard Castle have long known the story of the Smith brothers and that Wilfred, or Willie as he was known, survived.

World War I

But how that happened was largely unknown until local historian Peter Wise searched the recently digitized archives of the local newspaper, the Teesdale Mercury. In a minuscule item buried at the bottom of a long grey column came the answer: Queen Mary, wife of King George V, heard about the sacrifice of the brothers and intervened to send Willie home.

A century later, the news has stirred memories and inspired a mixture of pride and astonishment.

"To say it's been massive is probably not an understatement," said Trevor Brookes, the newspaper's editor. "Every parent can probably roughly imagine how terrible it would be to lose a son, but to lose five sons at the risk of losing a sixth—that's tragedy. I don't think any British family suffered a greater loss."

Some 9 million soldiers died in the war that began in 1914 and ended in 1918, and it was common for families to lose more than one son. Brothers and friends would join so-called "Pals Brigades" so they could serve together—and communities sometimes found that a single skirmish could wipe out a generation of their men.

But even so, this story was different.

Wilfred was the youngest son of a chimney sweep who scraped by in the slums of Barnard Castle, a market town nestled in a landscape dotted by herds of deer and turreted castles in northern England. When Wilfred was 12, there were 10 members of his family living in three rooms in Poor House Yard, according to the 1911 Census of England and Wales. While Wilfred was still in school, his 14-year-old brother, Frederick, was already working in a local mill.

For many poor young men, joining the army was an adventure, a chance to get regular meals and pay, especially since recruiters told them the war would be over in a matter of months. Local World War I buff John Pringle said the boys would have been anxious to leave the drudgery of the flax mill or the shoe-thread factory.

Wilfred didn't want to go, but did when his country called. A photograph taken at the time showed four of the brothers posing in their uniforms with a cute white dog at their feet. The image would remain on Margaret's mantel throughout the war.

Robert 22, died first, in September 1916. George Henry, 26, died less than two months later.

Frederick, 21, died in July 1917, while the eldest, 37-year-old John William Stout—who had their mother's maiden name because she was not yet married when he was born—died in October 1917. The fifth son, Alfred, died in July 1918.

Margaret's grief was apparently more than the vicar's wife, Sarah Elizabeth Bircham, could bear. Bircham, who organized care packages for troops in the trenches, wrote to Queen Mary about the deaths of Margaret's five sons and how she had a sixth son still at war.

The Teesdale Mercury reported what happened next, printing the reply of the queen's secretary, Edward Wallington.

"I am commanded by the queen to thank you for your letter of the 16th instant, and to request you to be good enough to convey to Mr. and Mrs. Smith of Bridgegate, Barnard Castle, an expression of Her Majesty's deep sympathy with them in the sad losses they have sustained by the death of their five sons.

"The Queen has caused Mr. and Mrs. Smith's request concerning their youngest son to be forwarded for consideration of the War Office authorities."

So Wilfred went home to Barnard Castle—though little is known about exactly how that came about. He suffered the lingering respiratory effects of a mustard gas attack and newspaper reports suggested he was temporarily blinded. But once home, he worked as a chimney sweep and a stone mason.

At the Bowes Museum, a memorial was erected to residents who fell in the Great War, including Wilfred's brothers. His mother laid the first wreath at its dedication in 1923—chosen by the war veterans for the honor. Wilfred was at her side.

He went on to become a devoted husband, father and grandfather who liked to laugh and took joy in simple things. His granddaughter, Amanda Nelson, recalls going to his home for lunch on weekends, where he would delight the little ones by racing snails or other bits of silliness.

His daughter Dianne Nelson said he doted on her and that, as the youngest, she got away with everything.

World War I

Now 70, she said her reserved father never talked about his experiences in the war, even when she needed to write a childhood essay on the topic and asked him to tell her about it. The family had heard about the queen and the letter, but it was simply a hazy oral tradition.

Amanda Nelson made a point of seeing the Steven Spielberg film, "Saving Private Ryan." The 1998 Oscar-winning film depicts the fictional account of a World War II rescue mission for a single American soldier whose brothers have been killed in the fighting.

"It was as if they knew the story of us—except they are called the Ryans and not the Smiths," she said.

Although Margaret Smith once told a relative "Don't have boys. They'll just end up being cannon fodder," Amanda Nelson stressed that Margaret believed she did the right thing by allowing her sons to serve.

"She would gladly send them again to fight," Amanda Nelson said. "For king and country."

In this community, where people often live not far from where their ancestors lived, the Smith story seems very real despite the passage of time. There's a sense of connection to the past that Brookes, the newspaper editor, feels strongly.

Earlier this month, he lifted a dusty, faded red book from an upstairs shelf that holds full-sized bound copies of the paper: the volume labeled 1918. He pushed his finger down the page, to the final sentences of a long column of newsprint, below an item on a produce sale for the War Prisoners Fund.

Brookes has wondered why such a unique and tragic tale would garner so little attention in the paper.

His guess was that by 1918, people had wearied of war—so many had lost so much. But he also speculated the plight of the Smith family might have been deemed less newsworthy because they were members of the town's underclass.

"If not for 'Private Ryan,' it might be lost to history," he said, crediting the Spielberg movie as having offered a contemporary connection.

Wilfred Smith lived until 1972, when he died at age 74. He was a frequent visitor to the monument at the Bowes Museum that bears his brothers' names.

Before 'Saving Private Ryan,' Pvt. Smith Was Saved

In "Saving Private Ryan," the now-older soldier stands before the graves of the men who saved him and recalls their sacrifice, saying he tried to live the best life he could. Wilfred Smith's family believes that he, too, could hold his head high as he scanned the names of his brothers at the Bowes obelisk.

"He was a good dad," Dianne Nelson said with pride. "He was a true person."

WORLD WAR I SPREAD FLOWERS AROUND TOO, AND NOT ONLY POPPIES

Portland, OR, USA

BOASTING SPECTACULAR VIEWS OF THE city skyline and—on a clear day—snow-covered Mount Hood, Portland's International Rose Test Garden in Washington Park is a refuge from a hectic world.

But during World War I, the rose garden offered a refuge of a different sort: It was a preserve for plants that European hybridists feared might be wiped out in the bombings.

While the rose garden did not become a reality until after the U.S. entered the war in 1917, it was proposed not long after the war began three years earlier.

World War I Spread Flowers Around Too, and Not Only Poppies

As early as August 1915, an Oregon newspaper reported that Jesse A. Currey, a Portland rose hobbyist, was working to gain support for his idea of a municipal rose test garden from American Rose Society President Wallace R. Pierson and Portland's George L. Baker, then the city's parks commissioner, and later its mayor when the garden was approved in 1917.

Currey got help from his friend George C. Thomas Jr., a rose enthusiast from Philadelphia and a captain in Army Air Service who flew in France during the war. In June 1918, the Oregonian newspaper called Thomas "America's greatest amateur rosarian," and reported that before he went to war, he left instructions that "as soon as the Portland garden was established, it should receive his two most promising seedlings."

In early 1918, the garden began receiving plants from growers in England and Ireland, as well as Los Angeles, Washington and the Eastern United States.

The garden is an example both of Oregon's support for the war through its natural resources—including food from its farms and timber from its forests—and as part of the era's City Beautiful movement, said Chet Orloff, director emeritus of the Oregon Historical Society.

"Through that whole period, we are really putting a lot of effort, at least this city is, into creating a greater parks system," said Orloff, who is president and director of Portland's Museum of the City. "The rose was such an important part of the persona of the city, and this was a great way to contribute to an international effort to preserve something."

Portland has long been nicknamed the "City of Roses." A decade before the test garden was proposed, 20 miles (32 kilometers) of Portland's streets were lined with rose bushes for the 1905 Lewis and Clark Centennial Exposition. Two years later Portland began its annual rose festival.

The test garden was a way to solidify the city's reputation as a rose-growing center internationally—its supporters at the time worried Seattle or Tacoma, Washington, could steal the title, according to the old newspaper accounts.

"This was still the era when cities were promoting themselves, and they did so by beautifying themselves," Orloff said.

World War I

In its first year, the garden occupied about a block, between a playground and an elk corral. Today, it spans 4.5 terraced acres (1.8 hectares), with more than 10,000 rose bushes—more than 600 varieties in every shape and color except black and blue, even stripes, said Harry Landers, the garden's curator.

Test beds are planted with new varieties evaluated on several characteristics, including disease resistance, bloom form, color and fragrance. A Gold Medal Garden features previous years' best selections, and the Shakespeare Garden features roses named after characters in the bard's works.

The flowers bloom from May until as late as November. Landers said about a half-million visitors from all over the world stop in to smell them each year.

"The fragrance is back into roses," Landers said, noting that some rose lovers had worried the smell had been bred out of them in favor of disease resistance. "The fragrance is just intoxicating."

They're most fragrant in the heat of the day, Landers said, though that's also when the garden is busiest. He said they're at their most beautiful in the morning, and he prefers the garden in the early mornings as the city below comes to life.

CULTURAL HERITAGE SO OFTEN ONE OF FIRST VICTIMS OF WAR

Leuven, Belgium

MARIE LEGRAND STILL HAS VISIONS of the horrid scene. Even the scent of smoke she smelled as a 3-year-old stings in her mind to this day.

"When I close my eyes like I do now, I see the whole city in front of me, and the flames," she told The Associated Press at her home, fanning invisible flames with her frail hands. A century later, she still remembers how German forces burned down the Leuven University library,

"The old Leuven, the old town, the old history. In short: History itself all went up in flames," she said of the Aug. 25, 1914, fire in the heart of the Belgian town east of Brussels.

World War I had started weeks earlier and Belgium had slowed Germany's march on France much more than expected. German irritation turned to anger, then to atrocities.

World War I

The destruction of the university library served little strategic purpose beyond ruining what people held dear—a practice that continues to thrive today, especially in the Middle East and Africa, where roaming rebels and defiant dictators are robbing the world of some of the highlights of human history.

"The strategy is destroying the identity of a community," said Leuven University archivist Mark Derez.

The torching of the Leuven University library drew international condemnation and was widely used in propaganda to purport that Germany lacked any civilized standards. Still, as shocking as it was a century ago, its example appears to have done nothing to check the practice of cultural vandalism during wartime.

"It is getting worse," said Joris Kila, a heritage protection expert. "And strangely enough, the worse it gets, the less money and determination there is to do something about it."

The 1954 Hague Convention for the Protection of Cultural Property in the Event of Armed Conflict makes it mandatory for signatory nations to ensure that such destruction does not happen. But many of today's conflicts rage in states with weak central governments and rebel forces that answer only to themselves.

In March 2001, the Taliban in Afghanistan dynamited the huge Bamiyan Buddhas, deeming them idolatrous and anti-Muslim. It was one of the regime's most widely condemned acts.

In 2012, Muslim extremists destroyed key parts of the heritage of the ancient Malian city of Timbuktu, razing tombs and burning ancient documents, saying they acted on divine orders. Similar actions have happened in Somalia and Iraq, where the Islamic State group destroyed holy shrines of other religions.

"You try to demoralize a local population. It is an attack on the identity of the population. It is an attack on the collective memory," Kila said.

In today's Leuven, the rebuilt university library displays a few of the charred books, sealed in glass cases and "serving as a kind of evidence for the German burning of the library," Derez said.

The printed letters that once combined into sentences and books of wisdom are now blackened beyond recognition, gone at the edges, curled up at the center.

Among the library's 300,000 lost books and manuscripts was the 16th century "Atlas of the human anatomy" by Andreas Vesalius, the founding father of that branch of science, a gift to the university from Emperor Charles V.

Derez said much evidence suggests that German forces wilfully destroyed the library to demoralize the people of Leuven, at the time a town of 42,500. The fires ultimately razed 1,081 of its 8,920 buildings.

"That kind of terror has something to do with reducing, assuring a minimum of civilian resistance during the invasion and a maximum of civilian cooperation during the occupation," he said.

It certainly worked on Legrand.

"Just talking about 'Germans' scared the kids," she said. To this day, at 103 years of age, Legrand said that "some residue of worry always remains."

When someone says they are German, it still gives her a small shock, she said.

"It should not be. But that's how it is," Legrand said.

If it leaves such an impression a century later, it is hardly surprising that demolishing monuments and cultural venues remains such a popular strategy. Even though individuals may run the risk of being prosecuted by the International Criminal Court in The Hague for such crimes, this rarely happens, Kila said.

"They all make promises, but at the end nobody puts their money where their mouth is by going out to arrest these people," he said.

WORLD WAR I AVIATION STILL ALIVE, AND SWOOPING, AT AERODROME IN NEW YORK

Rhinebeck, New York

THERE'S STILL A PLACE WHERE buzzing biplanes swoop in pursuit of German triplanes, where pilots in open cockpits let their scarves flutter in the wind.

The sights and sounds of World War I flight are recreated regularly at the Old Rhinebeck Aerodrome in New York's Hudson Valley, where an original American Curtiss JN-4H "Jenny" shares the sky with reproductions of a French Spad VII and German Fokkers.

"I get to shoot down a Fokker triplane every Sunday afternoon," said air show director Chris Bulko, who flew the Spad. "I call it playing with the toys here and sharing them with everybody else, and inviting them into our sandbox."

World War I Aviation Still Alive, and Swooping, at Aerodrome in New York

The aerodrome 80 miles north of New York City is one of the scattered places around the world that puts on air shows based on World War I. The attraction also boasts a museum and hangars packed with planes from the dawn of flight up to World War II. But the weekend air shows bring the crowds. Saturday shows highlight the early history of aviation. Sundays are devoted to WWI.

Men dressed in old-time overalls start balky engines with a hard pull down on propellers. Bulko blows kisses to the crowd on takeoff and chases a doppelganger of the Fokker triplane that was piloted by Manfred von Richthofen (a.k.a. the Red Baron). No machine guns here, though pilots show off their skill by flying through falling streams of toilet paper.

Back on the ground, a cartoony melodrama plays out involving Sir Percy Goodfellow, Trudy Truelove and the scheming villains. It's family entertainment harkening back to a perilous period.

Flying could be deadly for the young pilots, some of whom were teenagers. Planes were wood-framed, fabric-covered and flammable. Enemy pilots attacked with the sun behind them to blind their prey, sometimes amid barrages of anti-aircraft fire. Machine guns jammed. There were no parachutes.

"It's a dangerous business simply because the planes are not reliable, in many respects. They are also sometimes difficult to fly," said John H. Morrow Jr., an expert in WWI aviation who teaches history at the University of Georgia.

Many of the planes that made it through war were destroyed as surplus, a big reason why originals are so rare.

Aerodrome founder Cole Palen bought a few old planes in 1951 when a Long Island hangar at the site of Charles Lindbergh's trans-Atlantic takeoff made way for a shopping plaza. Palen collected pre-WWII planes for the rest of his life and reproduced hard-to-find historical planes, usually with original engines.

In 1960, he put on his first air show at an old farm he bought in the Hudson Valley. Though Palen died in 1993, the not-for-profit organization is now run by other vintage air buffs. Paid pilots and staff are helped by volunteers, many who are enamored of the comparatively clunky aircraft.

World War I

The Jenny, for instance, has a top speed of around 75 mph (23.89 Celsiu), but pilot and head mechanic Ken Cassens notes it had a "pretty advanced engine for its time" as he gave a post-flight tour of the plane.

"Building and maintaining and recovering airplanes, in a way, it's a lot of fun," Cassens said. "It's a lot of work, but it's enjoyable work.

WORLD WAR I: THE HORRORS OF WAR THAT INSPIRED INNOVATIVE ART

New York, United States

IN THE SUMMER OF 1914, with the war in Europe just two weeks old, Henry James knew that something had been lost forever.

"Black and hideous to me is the tragedy that gathers, and I'm sick beyond cure to have lived on to see it," the American author, an expatriate in London at the time, wrote to a friend. "You and I, the ornaments of our generation, should have been spared this wreck of our belief that through the long years we had seen civilization grow and the worst become impossible.... It seems to me to undo everything, everything that was ours, in the most horrible retroactive way."

James died in 1916, two years before the armistice was declared between the allies and the Germans, and the wreckage of World War I was beyond even his imagination. Millions were dead, empires dissolved, centuries-old beliefs upended. Many survivors wondered how the world had been caught up in a war fought not for any identifiable cause, but because no one knew how to stop it.

Prolonged conflicts destroy the worlds they were born in, and few did so as thoroughly and as terribly as World War I. Among writers, World War I changed both the stories they told and how they told them. Artists in general left behind an extraordinary legacy of painting, music, literature and film and many of the defining achievements of a movement, Modernism, that challenged our very identities and raised questions still being asked today.

"If you look at the 19th century, you have this whole notion of progress through technology — the notion of science, the increasing organization of society," says Jan Schall, an art historian and curator of modern and contemporary art at the Nelson-Atkins Museum of Art in Kansas City, Mo.

"What the war did was turn this ideal upside down. You had mass death through mass technological warfare — the use of chemicals, the use of machinery. And you see the impact on the kind of art that is being turned out, a sense of discontinuity and fragmenting."

World War I was unique for the art it inspired, and for the art's disillusion with war itself; winners and losers both despaired. In an essay, the literary critic Adam Kirsch notes that poetry had a history dating back to ancient Greece of treating war as a tragic, but essential rite of passage and proving ground. World War I broke the spell.

"Wars keep being fought, of course, but now they are justified on the grounds of necessity, self-defense, even human rights — never on the grounds that war itself is a splendid achievement or the true calling of men," Kirsch wrote.

Poets and writers on both sides of the Atlantic at first cheered on the battle. Carl Sandburg's "Four Brothers" hailed the "Ballplayers, lumberjacks, ironworkers, ready in khaki/A million, ten million, singing, 'I am ready.'"

The New York Society Library had an exhibit featuring releases from the British publisher, Wellington House, which specialized in a line of pro-war literature. Contributors included J.M. Barrie, Thomas Hardy and Arthur Conan Doyle, who met with troops in the spring of 1916 and completed "A Visit To Three Fronts" over the summer.

World War I: The Horrors of War that Inspired Innovative Art

"If there are pessimists among us they are not to be found among the men who are doing the work," Doyle wrote. "There is no foolish bravado, no underrating of a dour opponent, but there is a quick, alert, confident attention to the job in hand which is an inspiration to the observer. These brave lads are guarding Britain in the present. See to it that Britain guards them in the future!"

The war overran and destroyed the dream. The German artist and sculptor Kaethe Kollwitz turned out a series of deathly statues, woodcuts and posters. American painter John Singer Sargent also spent time at the front and responded with an epic testament to the crimes of war, the 20-foot-long (6 meters) painting "Gassed," in which blinded soldiers form a procession that mocks the ideal of military discipline.

Among anti-war poems, few were so bitter, or indelible, as the British poet Wilfred Owen's "Dulce et Decorum Est," with its wretched images and scorn for the venerable adage "Dulce et Decorum est pro patria mori": ("It is sweet and proper to die for your country").

> If you could hear, at every jolt, the blood
> Come gargling from the froth-corrupted lungs,
> Obscene as cancer, bitter as the cud
> Of vile, incurable sores on innocent tongues,
> My friend, you would not tell with such high zest
> To children ardent for some desperate glory,
> The old Lie; Dulce et Decorum est
> Pro patria mori.

In "A Farewell to Arms," Ernest Hemingway declared that "Abstract words such as glory, honor, courage, or hallow were obscene beside the concrete names of villages, the numbers of roads, the names of rivers, the numbers of regiments and the dates." T.S. Eliot's "The Hollow Men," one of the touchstones of post-war literature, sketches a ravaged, barren landscape:

> In this valley of dying stars
> In this hollow valley
> This broken jaw of our lost kingdoms

World War I

> In this last of meeting places
> We grope together
> And avoid speech
> Gathered on this beach of the tumid river

Soldiers returned maimed, traumatized, bewildered, a "lost generation," as Gertrude Stein called them. In Erich Maria Remarque's famous anti-war novel, "All Quiet On the Western Front," a German soldier rejects his patriotism, abandons his humanity and loses his life. Hemingway's short story "Soldier's Home" tells of a veteran named Krebs who finds that no one in his community wants to hear what really happened.

"Krebs found that to be listened to at all he had to lie and after he had done this twice he, too, had a reaction against the war and against talking about it," Hemingway wrote. "A distaste for everything that had happened to him in the war set in because of the lies he had told."

World War I was the last major conflict presided over by kings and Kaisers and the last to begin with even the pretense of old-fashioned rules of battle. Jean Renoir's "La Grande Illusion," released in 1937, was a classic portrait of how the war destroyed old beliefs in hierarchy and honor, embodied in the film by the bond between the aristocratic German captain played by Erich Von Stroheim and the captured French officer played by Pierre Fresnay.

The officers "were at home in the international sportsmanship of the prewar world, but the skills, maneuvers, courage and honor that made military combat a high form of sportsmanship are a lost art, a fool's game, in this mass war," The New Yorker's Pauline Kael later wrote of the film.

World War I was a severing of history, and a violation of logic, that justified the skepticism of Modernists who had questioned whether a book needed a beginning, middle and end, whether a song needed a melody, whether a picture needed to faithfully reproduce its subject—or even have a subject. James Joyce, Virginia Woolf and other Modernist authors rejected conventional narrative and grammar. Dadaist artists such as Marcel Duchamp and Hans Richter turned out jarring, surreal paintings, plays and sculptures that mirrored their feelings about the war, while composers such as Arnold Schoenberg and Alban Berg produced disjointed, "atonal" works.

World War I: The Horrors of War that Inspired Innovative Art

"War proved that everything was temporary, fleeting, and the art world reflected it," says Doran Cart, senior curator of the National World War I Museum in Kansas City. "And it helped inspire works of Modernism because the war itself was so modern and changed how people saw their communities and saw each other."

Ironically, one of the war's most enduring legacies was not a protest, but a call to service. In 1917, commercial artist James Montgomery Flagg was asked by the U.S. government to create a poster that would encourage young people to join the military. He sketched a furrowed, red-cheeked man with a starred top hat and white goatee, the face based in part on Flagg himself.

He added a simple caption: "I Want YOU For U.S. Army," shortened in popular memory to "UNCLE SAM WANTS YOU."

THE DAY FRANCE RELIED ON ITS CABBIES TO BOOST ITS WAR EFFORT

Paris, France

THE NEXT TIME YOU FLAG a taxi on a crowded city street, spare a thought for the cabbie—and perhaps consider a bigger tip.

Weeks after World War I erupted, with the capital under threat from German invaders, French military chiefs devised a novel way for soldiers to travel to the front lines: by taxi.

To that end, they requisitioned hundreds of cabs, and their drivers were charged with the risky mission of getting thousands of troops to the battlefield.

In September 2014, France honored the centennial of the "Taxis of the Marne," which have become the stuff of legend for millions of French school kids present and past. Paris City Hall, the Defense Ministry and

The Day France Relied on Its Cabbies to Boost Its War Effort

private company Alpha taxis had commemoration parades on Sunday that included taxis from the era.

Germany opened the Western Front on Aug. 4, sweeping into Belgium and hoping to overwhelm France before Russia had a chance to fully mobilize to the east. The lightning-fast Schlieffen plan aimed to bring German forces into Paris within weeks. After the guns of August blared, the French army looked as if it was on way to defeat.

On Sept. 6, 1914, Kaiser Wilhelm's troops were just a few dozen kilometers northeast of Paris. The French army requisitioned the taxis over two days to carry bedraggled troops returning from the collapsed front back to new battle lines. The call-up was part of a rising, nationwide war effort that also commandeered horses and called up more than three French million peasants to drop plowshares for guns.

Gen. Joseph Gallieni, the military governor of Paris who concocted the plan, ordered the taxis to gather on a grassy esplanade in front of the gold-domed Invalides military museum, which honors war victims and is the burial site of Napoleon Bonaparte. The commute to battle through the Paris environs must have been quite a sight: A rumbling caravan of hand-cranked red cars with bright yellow spokes packed a half-dozen soldiers behind primly-dressed drivers.

In that day, a motorcade was as much a technological innovation as unmanned drones might be considered in conflicts today.

For a bloody four-year war in which millions on both sides were mobilized, a few thousand troops didn't matter much at first sight. But the psychological impact on a nation used to "Belle Epoque" Paris comforts was critical. The French were beginning to seriously heed President Raymond Poincare's call for a "sacred union" of civilians and soldiers in the war effort.

"Taxi drivers were generally from modest backgrounds, so they represented the soul of Paris to some extent," said Laurent Lasne, author of a French book on the taxis. As for the soldiers, he said, "they were tired . . . The taxis were a rather nice surprise."

Time was of the essence. Train services were overloaded or unavailable. In came the taxis, mainly red Renault AG1s. They clocked an average 25 kilometers per hour (15 mph), according to the Web site of the national museum's authority.

Paris was in a siege mentality, with shops and restaurants facing a 9 p.m. curfew to close their doors. Checkpoints cropped up on the city's edges. The U.S. ambassador predicted the city would fall in 48 hours.

"Everybody thought that Paris was finished. Everybody thought that the Germans, if they had followed the roads straight, would run right into Paris," said Lasne. "Instead of heading straight to Paris, the Germans started moving to the east."

According to the French Senate's Web site, the soldiers crammed five to a vehicle in a caravan of about 1,100 taxis, amounting to "the first time that the automobile was used for military ends." That's a slight exaggeration: Lasne said only about 700 cabs were actually involved. Historians seem to agree that a total of about 5,000 soldiers took part.

Lasne also debunked some illustrations showing troops and taxis cheered in a thankful Paris. In fact, the vehicles were empty but for their drivers, until they reached the suburbs of Livry-Gargan and Gagny.

Once there, crowds did turn out. Mothers, sisters and spouses poured out into the streets of the towns along the route, cheering them on with dry sausage, bread and wine.

With British expeditionary troops at their side, the French scored their first victory of the war at Marne in September 1914, providing a moment of French euphoria and setting the stage for four years of devastating trench warfare.

Gallieni, who died before the four-year conflict ended, played up the courage and national fervor of the drivers.

"Once they understood the importance of the task they had to cooperate in, the taxi drivers displayed totally remarkable fervor," he wrote in his memoirs. "They felt proud of the service asked of them, and when I asked one if he wasn't afraid of the mortars, he responded: 'we'll do like our comrades, we'll go where we have to.'"

They nevertheless got paid, even if the penny-pinching War Ministry doled out less than one-third of the paycheck at the time. The rest was paid after the war was over.

THEY NEVER WILTED. POPPIES LIVE ON AS ENDURING SYMBOL OF THE WAR

London, England

WILLIAM SELLICK PINCHED THE TINY scarlet petals with deft ease, turning them into paper poppies and pressing them into a wreath.

The flowers are a potent symbol of remembrance and patriotism that sprang up in the aftermath of World War I to honor the war dead and raise funds for survivors. A century since the Great War, the poppies live on: They are hung as wreaths or worn on lapels across Britain—from Prime Minister David Cameron to X-Factor celebrities to countless commuters braving the blustery streets of London—each time the nation prepares to mark Armistice Day on Nov. 11.

Each handmade flower evokes the image of poppies springing up from destruction and decay in Belgium's Flanders Fields, home to many of the Great War's bloodiest battlefields. The haunting scene was immortalized in a war poem by Canadian army doctor John McCrae: "In Flanders fields the poppies blow/Between the crosses row on row."

McCrae noticed that the resilient red corn poppy was the first plant to flourish in the churned-up landscape. The poem, penned in 1915 shortly after McCrae buried a friend, struck a chord around the world and started poppy symbolism in the English-speaking world.

For Sellick, who suffered combat stress after an army tour to Northern Ireland in the 1970s, making poppies is a way to move on from a life shadowed by depression and alcoholism. He doesn't like to recall his army days, but every November he makes an effort to help plant crosses decorated with poppies outside London's Westminster Abbey.

"Most of the time when we go out to plant the poppy field it's wet and windy," he said with a laugh. "But I always make sure I do the plot for my regiment."

During the centenary of World War I, the poppy is more ubiquitous than ever. At the Tower of London in 2014, a crimson sea of ceramic poppies flooded the ancient moat in a stunning display titled "Blood Swept Lands and Sea of Red." A total of 888,426 ceramic flowers—each representing a British soldier who died during the war—were planted over the summer, with the last one to be placed on Armistice Day.

Although the poppy is most commonly worn today in Britain and Commonwealth countries like Canada, Australia, and New Zealand, it was a woman from the U.S. state of Georgia who was responsible for turning it into a symbol of the Great War. Moina Michael, a teacher, was so moved by McCrae's poem that she vowed always to wear a poppy as a way to "keep the faith with all who died."

Michael started to give poppies to ex-servicemen in New York, where she worked, and the American Legion adopted her idea of selling handmade poppies to raise money for wounded ex-servicemen in 1918. A Frenchwoman soon brought the practice to Britain, where the Royal British Legion began the tradition of a "Poppy Appeal" to help those returning from the war.

The British Army major credited with opening the first factory employing wounded vets as poppy makers had his doubts early on.

"I do not think it can be a great success but it is worth trying," George Howson wrote in a letter to his parents in 1922.

They Never Wilted. Poppies Live on as Enduring Symbol of the War

To this day, the factory in west London's Richmond makes the bulk of the 45 million poppies, wreaths and crosses sold across Britain. Full-time workers like Sellick assemble each by hand year round, though most of the poppies don‹t appear until late October, when they adorn war memorials up and down the country and are sold on virtually every street corner.

Many of the wreaths are featured on Remembrance Sunday, the second Sunday in November, when Queen Elizabeth II leads an annual tribute at London's Cenotaph to all those who died in World War I and later conflicts.

As time passes, veterans' groups face the challenge to keep the poppy—and the memories it stands for—relevant and meaningful to a new generation.

Ann Butler, a teacher, was among the many parents who brought their children to see the poppies at the Tower of London.

"They know some of my relatives were in the war. For them to see this, to know that each flower represents someone who died, makes it all more real," she said. "As the generations go on, there will inevitably be less of a connection."

There are also those in Britain who avoid the tradition, saying the poppy has become too politicized and nationalistic, or even a symbol that glorifies war. Margaret MacMillan, a historian at Oxford University, said she once reluctantly pinned a poppy when appearing on television because producers insisted she do so.

"There is tremendous pressure for people to wear them," she said. "Symbols can be useful but you need much more. There's more to memory than popping it on once a year and forgetting about it."

IN 1914 AMID THE GREAT WAR, THE GREATEST OF CHAMPAGNE VINTAGES

Epernay, France

DEEP IN THE LABYRINTHINE CELLARS of the Pol Roger Champagne house, rows of century-old bottles caked in mold bear testimony to perhaps the greatest, and surely the most heroic of vintages.

As champagne goes, 1914 was a superlative year when the warmest of summers left the richest of grapes. As war goes, gunfire could be heard just beyond the hills and most men were off fighting in the horrors of World War I.

Yet, even in those dark days, France without champagne would simply not be France. And somehow, the heady mix produced a vintage for the ages in which dedication beat fear.

If the usual harvesters had turned into soldiers, there were women, old men, and sometimes even children to take their place. They picked and pressed in the face of German enemy fire to produce a drink which is still celebrated over a century later.

"Those who were still in town went into the vineyards. Even the schools were closed," said Hubert de Billy, the great grandson of Maurice Pol-Roger, the wartime mayor of Epernay, which along with Reims is the heart of champagne production. "Obviously everybody was scared. There was bombing all around."

The war hit the Champagne region hard and it was not only the wine industry that suffered. In Reims, the Notre Dame cathedral, one of world's greatest Gothic treasures, was badly bombed in an act of cultural destruction that helped turn international opinion against Germany.

For the citizens of Champagne, some weeks were so tough that all they could do was seek refuge underground. And Champagne houses obliged—opening their cellars, many going 100 feet (30 meters) below the earth. School was held, mothers gave birth and some denizens used chalk to scrawl graffiti in endless subterranean corridors now owned by the Taittinger champagne house.

"The soft chalk was ideal to express a strong emotion," company president Pierre-Emmanuel Taittinger said of the scratches, some depicting pointed German helmets.

Above ground, it was not only the honor of a nation that was at stake but, just as importantly, the livelihood of a whole region. The winegrowers dealt in the effervescence of joy at a time of moral desolation, yet they had no choice.

"It is the purpose of the city," said de Billy. "Even the lawyers are devoted to champagne. Without champagne, the life of the town is gone. It was the same in the war."

That sense of purpose pushed his great-grandfather, mayor Maurice, to go all out for the 1914 vintage even though the town had briefly fallen to the Germans and war was still in earshot. Maurice even printed his own "currency" to pay pickers, assuring them they could turn them in for real francs after the war.

Even in times of desperation, wine growers looked beyond the immediate. The great vintage was only to be ready for drinking a decade later, when, they imagined correctly, the war would be won.

World War I

"The 1914 is a vintage that has been picked at the sound of bullets and drunk at the sound of trumpets," said de Billy.

Even in those days, the lore of champagne was already well established. Winston Churchill had been a devoted fan of Pol Roger since 1906, de Billy said, and later in life the British leader famously said "Remember, gentlemen, it's not just France we are fighting for, it's Champagne!"

Americans, too, had already found the love of fizz. Poet Alan Seeger, the uncle of folk singer Pete, has become a favorite subject for Taittinger, who celebrates him with a plaque decorated with the verses at the family's chateau just outside Epernay.

Seeger was looking for the bohemian life in Paris but ended as a volunteer for France in the Great War. He died on the Western Front close to Champagne in 1916, but not before writing an ode to the "sweet wine of France that concentrates/The sunshine and the beauty of the world."

Seeger already mourned "those whose blood, in pious duty shed/Hallows the soil where that same wine had birth."

Even now it jars how close the horrors and joys of life stand side by side. Past the last vineyards close to Reims, cemeteries and monuments dot the landscape where thousands of crosses, German and French, stand with the same precision as the long rows of vines.

For Pol Roger, it is also that interplay of triumph and tragedy which must be savored in a rare remaining 1914 bottle.

The taste is nothing like the full, yet crisp taste of the 2004 vintage.

"The bubbles that you know when you pour a glass have disappeared," said de Billy. "The taste will be more coffee, more chocolate. To give you an image, it will be more like a Madeira or a Sherry."

Yet even one century later, de Billy has to acknowledge the vintage is still strong enough to show its origins.

"You can feel a bit of fizziness on the tongue."

WORLD WAR I:
A REMEMBRANCE IN PICTURES

A re-enactor dressed in a World War One uniform stands guard outside the Prowse Point Cemetery in Ploegsteert, Belgium, July 22, 2010.

The grave of Belgian World War I soldier Max Pelgrims at the cemetery of Laeken, Belgium, January 13, 2014. He died on August 19, 1914, just weeks after war was declared.

A re-enactor dressed as a World War I British Cavalry soldier makes a charge during a performance at the Memorial Museum Passchendaele in Zonnebeke, Belgium, August 17, 2014. Various re-enactment groups participated in a weekend of World War I activities for the general public.

Soldiers stand next to a restored B-type (B2737) WWI bus outside the Menin Gate during a Last Post ceremony in Ypres, Belgium, September 20, 2014. The B2737 is one of four surviving B-type buses in known existence.

A statue of three soldiers at the World War I Navarin Memorial in Souain-Perthes-les-Hurlus, France, Wednesday, October 14, 2014. Located in the spot where the Battle of Champagne raged, the monument commemorates the fighting of Oct. 1914 and Sept. 1915. The memorial depicts three patrolling soldiers in the guise of General Gouraud, Lieutenant Quentin Roosevelt, son of U.S. President Theodore Roosevelt who died in 1918 in the Tardenois and the brother of the sculptor who fell on the Chemin des Dames.

World War I graves are illuminated by candles at the Tyne Cot Commonwealth cemetery in Zonnebeke, Belgium, October 17, 2014. The event, known as the "Light Front," was organized around several WWI battle sites in Belgium to commemorate 100 years since the start of the First World War.

Crowds watch a remembrance day ceremony at the near completed ceramic poppy art installation by artist Paul Cummins entitled 'Blood Swept Lands and Seas of Red' in the dry moat of the Tower of London in London, November 11, 2014.

The statue of a French Poilu in front of the Douaumont Ossuary in Verdun, France, April 3, 2017. World War I saw unprecedented trench warfare in Northern France and Belgium.

The bones of soldiers are piled up in a crypt at the Douaumont Ossuary in Verdun, France, April 3, 2017. The toll of dead so immense in the Verdun region that soldiers from both sides were buried together in the ossuary.

Buglers play the Last Post as the sun rises during an ANZAC Day dawn service at Polygon Wood Buttes New British Cemetery in Zonnebeke, Belgium, April 25, 2017. ANZAC Day is a national day of remembrance in Australia and New Zealand that broadly commemorates all Australians and New Zealanders who served in all wars.

New Zealand soldiers watch 'From the Uttermost Ends of the Earth' on October 11, 2017 as it is projected onto the Menin Gate during a commemoration of the WWI Battle of Passchendaele. In October of 1917 the New Zealand division suffered heavy losses during the Third Battle if Ypres.

Grave stones at Thiepval Memorial, northern France, during a military-led vigil to commemorate the 100th anniversary of the beginning of the Battle of the Somme one of the deadliest chapters of World War I, June 30, 2016.

A CENTURY LATER, BRITISH ARMY HONORS SOLDIERS KILLED IN WWI

Loos-en-Gohelle, France

SCOTSMAN WILLIAM MCALEER HAD BEEN in France barely two months when, just before sunrise on Sept. 25, 1915, he was among thousands of other troops who launched the British army's largest attack so far of World War I.

By the next day, the 22-year-old private from a seaside town in Fife was dead. Almost 60,000 British troops died in the Battle of Loos, and a third disappeared with no known grave.

McAleer was one of them, until nearly a century later, when workers building a new prison turned up his remains in a common grave.

On Friday, March 14, 2014 McAleer, and 19 other still unidentified British soldiers, were reburied with full military honors in a ceremony in the sleepy northern French village, close to where they fell in battle. The ceremony was a reminder of the horrors of a war that devastated this continent 100 years ago—and as a reminder of why many Europeans today are so wary of seeing a new conflict on their eastern flank in Ukraine.

A bagpiper played "Amazing Grace" as McAleer's coffin was carried through the fog-shrouded cemetery Friday morning by six Royal Regiment of Scotland soldiers wearing kilts. A distant relative of McAleer's, Stephen McLeod, represented McAleer's family at the funeral.

"He was my great uncle. My gran gave me his Mass card when I joined the army," said McLeod, 47, of Cowdenbeath, Fife.

"In the centenary year (of the start of the war), to be able to remember those who've fallen, and for it be your kith and kin, how can you find the words?" McLeod said after the ceremony.

Around 200 people, some from as far away as Australia, turned out for the hour-long ceremony. Many were history buffs who'd heard about the ceremony on the website of the Western Front Association, a historical society.

"We've been doing this for 30 years," said Iris Oakey, an Englishwoman who attended with her brother, John Mawson. Their grandfather fought further north on the Western Front at Ypres in Belgium. Together they've visited World War I sites in over a dozen countries. "Every cemetery has a story, every single one," Oakey said.

The Battle of Loos was a failed attempt to break through the German line. It was memorialized in English poet Robert Graves' autobiography "Good-bye to All That." Rudyard Kipling's son John also died here, and is buried at another British cemetery nearby. It was Kipling who proposed the phrase "Known Unto God" for unidentifed casualties that is engraved on limestone tombstones across the Western Front.

First World War remains still turn up regularly, during construction projects or in the spring planting season. More than 700,000 soldiers killed in the Great War were never found, their remains now part of the earth along the 600-kilometre-long (360-mile-long) route of the Western Front.

In January of 2014 a nearly complete skeleton of an unidentified French soldier was unearthed at the Memorial of Verdun, where construction is underway on renovations to mark the centenary of the war. Remains of 26 French soldiers have also been found in Fleury-devant-Douaumont, one of France's "ghost villages" that were entirely destroyed by the war. And in

2012, another French soldier's remains turned up during construction of a canal that stretches 100 kilometres (60 miles) along the old Western Front.

What makes McAleer's case especially notable is that unlike most of these other cases, investigators were able to reach back through history and give him a name, a history, and now, a proper grave.

In October 2010, workers building a new prison a few miles east of Loos-en-Gohelle turned up the remains. They were found along with 19 other British and 30 German soldiers, carefully laid out in a common grave that investigators determined was dug by the German side, based on where the front line had then run.

McAleer was identified by investigators working for the Commonwealth War Graves Commission, or CWGC, thanks to an ID tag found with his remains. Efforts to identify the others were unsuccessful, although investigators were able to trace half of them to a specific regiment. Their graves, like the majority of the graves in Loos' British cemetery, will bear the epitaph "Known Unto God."

The German remains were handed over to VDK, the German war graves body, which has been working to identify them.

Members of the Royal Regiment of Scotland's 2nd Battalion, the modern-day descendants of McAleer's Royal Scottish Fusiliers, were on hand for the March 14, 2014 ceremony to honor their fallen comrades. Representatives of regiments for the other 10 soldiers whose regiments could be traced also participated.

Carl Liversage, a CWGC official based in France, said, "You can't describe the feeling of finding the casualty and seeing the headstone and saying 'I think I made a difference.'"

CHRISTMAS 1914: THE DAY EVEN WORLD WAR I SHOWED HUMANITY

Ploegsteert, Belgium

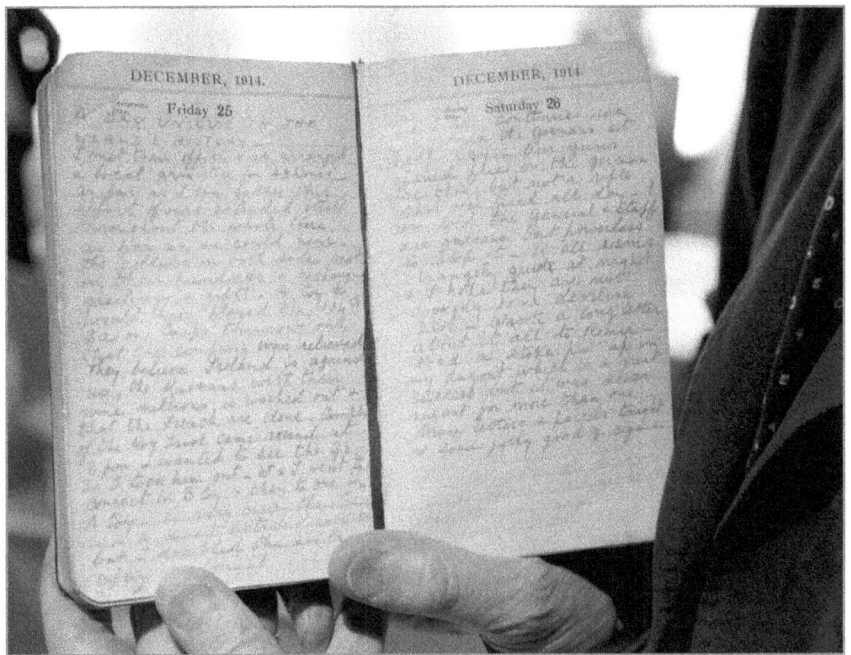

WITH BRITISH AND GERMAN FORCES separated only by a no-man's land littered with fallen comrades, sounds of a German Christmas carol suddenly drifted across the frigid air: "Stille Nacht, Heilige Nacht" ("Silent Night, Holy Night").

Then, during that first Christmas Day in World War I, something magical happened.

Soldiers who had been killing each other by the tens of thousands for months climbed out of their soggy, muddy trenches to seek a shred of humanity amid the horrors of war.

Hands reached out across the narrow divide, presents were exchanged, and in Flanders Fields a century ago, a spontaneous Christmas truce in 1914 briefly lifted the human spirit.

"Not a shot was fired," Lt. Kurt Zehmisch of the 134th Saxony regiment wrote with amazement in his diary that Christmas.

On the other side of the front line, Pvt. Henry Williamson of the London Rifle Brigade was amazed by the goodwill among his enemies. "Yes, all day Xmas Day & as I write. Marvelous, isn't it?"

Few could be believe their eyes, especially on this mud-caked patch of Belgium and northern France where crimson poppies had long ago shriveled in the cold.

Peace allowed for corpses to be recovered from the fields and given a proper burial. Fighting continued in many other places on the front line. But it was a momentary peace in a war that would last for nearly four more years.

THE BIRDCAGE

Near one of the spots where British and German soldiers fraternized for the unexpected truce, a dark, dirt track veers off the road and meanders into the gloom of the woods.

There, a cleared space has the graves of British soldiers who died on Dec. 19, 1914, in a battle as gruesome as it was insignificant, their dreams of a peaceful Christmas ignored and buried in the cold mud.

It was a time when swift military movement from Germany across France to the Belgian coast was grinding to a stalemate, leaving hundreds of thousands of casualties behind. For both sides—Germany versus an alliance led by France and Britain—this buried any hope that the war would be over by Christmas.

The result was a form of warfare across trenches where human life was expendable.

"There are a number of local attacks which never make it into the history books, but which all cause a great loss among the troops," said Piet Chielens, curator at the In Flanders' Fields Museum in Ypres, Belgium.

The Dec. 19, 1914 "Birdcage" attack occurred on a bulge of the German line about the size of a football (soccer) field. Allied soldiers also had been thinking about Christmas, but for 80 of them it turned into disaster in an area where a warren of barbed wire had given the German defenders a huge advantage.

Chielens said that during those early days of the war both sides dug into the Flemish soil, with commanders "attacking without deep thought, without deep concern about the fate of their men." The infamous "Birdcage" was one of those battles that made them realize that strategy wouldn't work.

With offensive artillery nearly non-existent and sometimes so wayward that it also was a threat to its own troops, soldiers were thrown into action where one machine gun could mow down a whole row of approaching men.

Some of the bodies found after the attack were so mangled they could no longer be told apart, and today the headstones of several casualties stand shoulder to shoulder to mark that horror.

"WE NO SHOOT"

Little wonder so many soldiers were pining for a glimmer of hope on Christmas Eve.

Frank and Maurice Wray of the London Rifle Brigade settled in to keep watch when they suddenly heard a German band in the trenches play songs "common to both nations," they later wrote in an article. "Quite understandably a wave of nostalgia passed over us."

At dawn, a German called out, "We good. We no shoot," and the Wrays noted: "And so was born an unofficial armistice." Men walked out, extremely apprehensive at first, many fearing some deadly trick. Then human warmth cracked the freezing cold.

Chielens said that similar scenes occurred at about 30 scattered points across many miles (kilometers) of Belgium. Others happened across the Western Front, which ran from the North Sea to the Swiss border.

Apart from talk in a shared language or merely with hands and kindred eyes, the men exchanged gifts, using everything from bully beef and barrels of beer to small mementos. Some played football.

German soldier Werner Keil scribbled his name on a piece of paper and gave a uniform button to 19-year-old British Cpl. Eric Rowden of the Queen's Westminster Rifles on Christmas Day 1914. "We laughed and joked together, having forgotten war altogether," Rowden wrote.

War, though, was never far away, including memories of the Birdcage still lingered and the burials of dead soldiers. It was hardly as if gunfire stopped all over to make room for warm embraces.

On the Belgian stretch around Ploegsteert alone, "we still have over 250 people dying on Christmas Day itself. There was enough fighting going on," Chielens said.

Despite the uplifting moment, commanders away from the trenches abhorred the softening of posture and fighting spirit. Cpt. Robert Hamilton of Britain's 1st battalion Royal Warwickshire noted: "I am told the general and staff are furious—but powerless to stop it."

25TH DECEMBER 1917

All that would change soon enough, and the 1914 truce would not be repeated.

Once British Gen. Sir Horace Smith-Dorrien had heard of it on Dec. 27, 1914, he wrote in a confidential memorandum that "this is only illustrative of the apathetic state we are gradually sinking into." He threatened disciplinary action to avoid a repeat.

"It was certainly remembered by the army commands because around Christmas in 1915, 1916, 1917, they see to it that there is no such thing as a truce possible because then the shelling will be deliberate and very intensive."

One thing did continue—the relentless killing.

Next to a monument in Ploegsteert to mark football playing at Christmas is the Prowse Point Military cemetery. Amid the 225 dead, three headstones from the 27th Battalion Australian infantry stand out.

Date of death? "25th December 1917."

A LANDSCAPE SHAPED BY WAR

Belgium and France

A CENTURY ON, THE FOUR SEASONS bring constant changes to the scarred landscapes and ruins of the First World War battlefields in Belgium and France.

Spring has its red poppies; summer its sun-kissed green foliage; fall stuns with vibrant colors; and winter brings the bleakness of rain and mud.

Soldiers of the 1914-1918 Great War had precious little time to appreciate the color. Instead they endured the mud as relentless shelling destroyed woods and villages and created desolate treeless landscapes, while many cities were reduced to heaps of rubble.

One hundred years on the force of nature has slowly changed these haunted places, yet many of the relics still exist, both above and below the surface. Some bunkers have turned into stables; shell craters became drinking

World War I

ponds for cattle. Many trenches and tunnels remain largely untouched on what was known as the Western Front, a battle line stretching from Belgium to the Swiss border.

Each vista offers a different view to the relic hunter. A road that seems to yield nothing in summer due to heavy foliage unveils a trove of treasures in the desolate winter. The Ziegler Bunker in Boezinge, Belgium, is likely one of the best preserved on the Ypres Salient, and the line of bunkers on Aubers Ridge in France give the viewer an idea of how important high ground was in the First World War.

A CENTURY LATER, A MYTHIC THUD OF A FOOTBALL IN WARTIME IS STILL HEARD

Ploegsteert, Belgium

ON THE SIDE OF A WINDSWEPT FIELD filled with scorpion weed, a simple wooden cross marks a unique event in football history.

At its base, amid wreaths of poppies, lie a smattering of balls and various club pennants, all in remembrance of the Christmas Truce of 1914.

A century ago on Christmas Day, German and British enemies left their World War I trenches and headed into no man's land in a few scattered locations on the Western Front for an unofficial truce among soldiers. Some eyewitness accounts say they were highlighted by something as remarkable as a few football kickabouts.

"Suddenly a Tommy came with a football," wrote Lt. Johannes Niemann of Germany, referring to a British soldier. "Teams were quickly established for a match on the frozen mud, and the Fritzes beat the Tommies 3-2."

If not fully-fledged matches, other soldier's diaries and various reports also spoke of balls being kicked about in friendship.

"A huge crowd was between the trenches. Someone produced a little rubber ball so of course a football match started," Lt. Charles Brockbank of the British Cheshire Regiment wrote in his diary, which is part of "The Greater Game" exhibit at the National Football Museum in Manchester.

The proponents of the sport have cherished that day as historic proof that there is little that can better bridge man's differences than football.

For Christmas 2014, the British supermarket chain Sainsbury's took the idea and turned it into a blockbuster ad, showing opposing soldiers living the truce amid a football match at the center of the heart-tugging, some say sanitized, view of that Great War day.

It is that unique mood of brotherhood that UEFA President Michel Platini used to unveil a Christmas truce monument on the former battlegrounds known as Flanders Fields in western Belgium, scene of some of the most horrendous killing in warfare.

"Together, they performed simple acts of reconciliation, culminating in the discovery of a shared language: football," Platini wrote to European Union leaders.

For those involved, it was most of all a yearning for a sense of normalcy, however momentarily, that pushed them over the edge of their trenches, unarmed.

The war had started on Aug. 4 when the German invasion of Belgium kicked off a series of events which quickly pit the German and Austro-Hungarian empires against Britain, France, Russia and several allies.

Germany swept into most of Belgium and northern France and even threatened Paris before the frontline was settled. Armies entrenched themselves for most of the next four years. At the time, though, the prevailing expectation on both sides had been to be home for Christmas.

When that didn't happen, an early sense of euphoria quickly made way for unrelenting gloom. It set the stage for the Christmas truce and those magic kickabouts.

Football players themselves had been involved in the fighting from the early days. Of the 5,000 professional players at the time, about 2,000 joined the armed forces. Sometimes whole lineups signed up at the same time to create what became known as the Footballers' Battalions. London club Clapton Orient, now known as Leyton Orient, alone had about 40 players and staff joining the war effort, all following the steps of their team captain.

Scotland's top team at the time, Edinburgh club Hearts, had its whole team join the British army one month ahead of that Christmas, a move which inspired others to join, Peter Francis of the Commonwealth War Graves Commission said. Christmas truce or not, seven members of that team were killed in the war.

One of the first footballers killed in the war was Larrett Roebuck, a Huddersfield defender. After playing for his team in a 1-0 victory at Leicester Fosse early in the 1914-15 season, he left for the Western Front and was killed in action on the eve of the first Battle for Ypres, a few kilometers from that patch of land in Ploegsteert.

"The story is that he set off running across the field with the machine guns going," said Roebuck's grandson, Frank Wood. "His friend saw him go down but he couldn't stop to help him. With the fight like that, you couldn't stop."

FIRST GAS ATTACKS UNLEASHED NEW HORRORS AND CHANGED WARFARE

Steenstrate, Belgium

AS A SPRING BREEZE WAFTED into his trench, commander Georges Lamour of the French 73rd infantry saw something almost surreal drift his way. A yellow-green cloud.

He barely had time to react. "All my trenches are choked," Lamour cried into the field telephone to headquarters. "I am falling myself!"

These were the last words heard from Lamour. World War I, and warfare itself, were never the same.

Chlorine gas—sent crawling in favorable winds over Flanders Fields from German positions—sowed terror and agony for the first time on April 22, 1915. The era of chemical weaponry had dawned. The weapon of mass slaughter came to symbolize the ruthlessness and, many say, futility of the 1914-1918 Great War.

"It is a new element in warfare. It is indiscriminate," said Piet Chielens, curator at the In Flanders' Fields Museum in nearby Ypres. And what's more, he said, "you create psychological terror."

Foaming at the mouth, crazed and blinded, the French soldiers fled in all directions—sucking for oxygen, finding poison instead. The chlorine seeped into body fluids and ate away at eyes, throat and lungs. Some 1,200 French soldiers were killed in the chaos of that first 5-minute gas attack and the fighting that followed. Lamour, like scores of comrades, was never found.

"You drown in your own lungs," Chielens said.

Today, cyclists crisscross these same fields and farmers plow around monuments honoring the first gas victims.

"NOTHING TO REPORT"

On the eve of the attack, German forces gathered their best and brightest at army headquarters in Tielt, some 30 miles (50 kilometers) behind the front line, for a momentous discussion.

Commanders had already been waiting 10 days for favorable winds, huddled in a patrician mansion lined with maps and dotted with landscape models. Tension had steadily risen after the Schlieffen Plan to smash through Belgium and take Paris by storm bogged down in Flanders and northern France. Germany was bent on breaking the stalemate of trench warfare. All options were open.

Holding back some German commanders was their sense of military honor. Some argued that deploying more troops would achieve a bigger breakthrough.

Fritz Haber, a chemical expert and future winner of the Nobel Prize in Chemistry, preached for more gas for more shock and awe. Others wondered if gas could be trusted to work as advertised.

Exasperated, Chief of General Staff Erich von Falkenhayn decided: Tomorrow we use the gas, or not at all.

Across the line, Lamour's French forces were reporting from the trenches: "Rien a signaler"—nothing to report. That might have been different had they been able to peer a bit further across no-man's land—at how German troops had dug in, under cover of night, more than 5,000 gas cylinders with tubes pointing their way.

The next morning, German trenches were filled with soldiers ready to pounce once the gas had cleared. The plan was to release the chlorine in the frosty morning hours, when it would cling best to the surface and give soldiers a full day to advance. But a windless morning came and went. The breeze picked up only in the afternoon. At 5 p.m. the gas cylinders were opened, with devastating effect.

Once the gas cleared, the soldiers jumped out and made more progress than they had in months. Men, horses, rats, even insects—all lay dead or choking before them.

"The effect of that gas was enormous," said historian Ann Callens. "Even the German troops and certainly the German generals were completely astonished."

"In one hour's time, they had a gap of more than 6 kilometers (4 miles) So the town of Ypres was nearly in their hands," said Callens, author of "Gas! Ieper 1915, the first gas attack."

Dusk was closing in fast though and lack of full confidence in gas came to haunt the Germans that day.

"The German army command has no great belief in this new weapon," Chielens said. "So they don't have a big infantry division behind it. That is not enough to result in a complete breakthrough."

After April 22, the surprise factor evaporated and the stalemate endured.

"IT SEEMS PRETTY CERTAIN WE SHALL RETALIATE"

But the genie was out of the bottle. The Germans needed only to look at how the prevailing westerly winds bent Flanders' stately trees toward their own positions to know that gas would inevitably come drifting their way. They could celebrate a momentary victory, but the war was about to become a lot uglier for both sides.

Laurence Cadbury of the British chocolate dynasty had come to Flanders to help as an ambulance driver. Cadbury, a pacifist Quaker, had an immediate grasp of what the Germans' use of the gas horror meant.

"It seems pretty certain we shall retaliate," he wrote to his parents only one week after the initial German attack. "After all, it is no use appealing to anyone."

The first use by allied forces came in September, when the British unleashed poison gas on the Germans at the battle of Loos, just across from Ypres in northern France.

Rival armies ultimately launched 146 gas attacks in Belgium, which covered only a small patch of the Western Front. The Germans used about 150 tons of gas in their first attack. Germany ultimately used 68,000 tons. The Allies used even more: 82,000 tons.

The lethal power of more sophisticated gases increased the horror by the month, even as the improvement of gas mask designs required more and more poison to be deployed. The invention of gas shells fired by artillery eliminated dependence on favorable winds.

The last gas attack came just three days before the armistice of Nov. 11, 1918. Historians estimate that more than 1 million soldiers were exposed to gas—and 90,000 killed.

"MON BIEN CHER GEORGES"

Peace brought no end to the suffering caused by the weapon.

"A lot of the effects did not kill you but they were lasting. You have chronic bronchitis, pneumonia," Chielens said. "The veterans of the war took it with them to their graves."

Dormant shells littered farmland. Even today, farmers suffer health problems after digging up this toxic harvest.

The French army told Georges Lamour's wife, Angele, that he either died from gas or was taken prisoner. She kept believing her husband was alive.

Month after month, she wrote letters to "Mon bien cher Georges." On May 2, 1918, three years after his presumed death, she still wrote: "Is springtime coming so late for you as it is for us?"

Sometimes, their three children took to pen and paper.

Lamour's son Etienne wrote on Dec. 8, 1915: "Mon cher papa, Mama allowed me to write you today because I came in first in the school exams, first in the division's literary contest, and second in German."

VICTOR IN THE BOSTON MARATHON ONE YEAR, A VICTIM OF WORLD WAR I THE NEXT

Vlamertinge, Belgium

AT THE VLAMERTINGE MILITARY CEMETERY in Flanders Fields, the headstone of James Duffy usually stands unnoticed among the solemn rows.

But one century after his death in 1915 and in the days leading up to the 2015 Boston Marathon, Duffy's grave has been honored with a scattering of wooden memento crosses, the drawing of an athlete, and a running bib.

"Died fighting for liberty—Ex-long distance champion runner of Scotland" is chiseled in stone. Yet to his family, what stands out is Duffy's win in the 1914 Boston Marathon and his death one year later, almost to the day, amid some of the worst violence of World War I.

Victor in the Boston Marathon One Year, a Victim of World War I the Next

One hundred years later, Maureen Kiesewetter donned bib No. 23149 and ran the Boston Marathon in honor of her great-great uncle.

"Last year we were able to celebrate his win. This year we will remember his passing and his sacrifice," she said.

Anyone with a love of running and a zest for living should consider the heroic and Olympian life and times of James "Jimmy" Duffy.

"He was quite a character," Kiesewetter said in a telephone interview from her home in Peoria, Illinois. She learned about Duffy from her grandmother when, at 27, she was preparing for her first marathon. "I was absolutely excited. Wow! How neat. I had no idea."

By that age, the whirlwind life of Duffy was already over. It started in Sligo, Ireland, before touching Edinburgh in Scotland, Canada and Boston before ending back across the ocean in the trenches of western Belgium, where shrapnel ripped his skull open.

"He was asking for his mother at the end," Kiesewetter said. During his 24 years he lived at full throttle, with running embedded in his blood.

After spending his youth in Ireland and Scotland, Duffy decided to try his luck in Canada where he quickly made a name for himself running. At 22 he was spearheading Canada's marathon effort at the 1912 Stockholm Olympics.

Because of the extreme heat that day, he set off too slowly and let the eventual medalists slip out of reach. He was still fresh when he crossed in fifth place, out of the medals but still good enough for some Olympic glory.

His best came at the 1914 Boston Marathon, with a performance that entered the lore of the race. In the closing stages of another sweltering day, Duffy was ahead with fellow Canadian Edouard Fabre, and the two exchanged the lead no less than four times before Duffy won by the smallest margin in the history of the race at the time, 15 seconds.

Famously, he asked for a beer and a cigarette after crossing the finish line. "That sounds like one of ours. He enjoyed a good time," Kiesewetter said.

Those 15 seconds still make it into the top 15 of tightest Boston Marathons ever. The road of professional racing lay open for him—but for the war.

On 28 June 1914, Archduke Franz Ferdinand of Austria was killed in Sarajevo, and the whole world was sucked into the Great War, including Duffy. "Within six months, he joined the army," Kiesewetter said. Canada was part of the British Commonwealth and soon he was back on a boat to Europe, this time to fight the Germans.

On April 22, 1915, Duffy found himself deployed in the Ypres Salient, scene for some of the worst fighting of the entire four-year war. That day, Germany opened the taps on more than 5,000 cylinders of chlorine gas, the first large-scale use of chemical weapons in warfare.

"He went in like a lot of young people not knowing what this was going to be about," Kiesewetter said.

Hundreds died that evening from gas and artillery, and Duffy's battalion was sent in for a counterattack. Frederick Scott, a poet and senior chaplain to Canadian forces, was inspecting the post-battle carnage by moonlight when he saw something move.

"I called out, 'Is anybody there?' A voice replied, 'Yes sir, there is a dying man here.'" It was Duffy. "He had been struck by a piece of shrapnel in the head and his brain was protruding," Scott wrote in his account "The Great War As I Saw It."

"We tried to lift him, but with his equipment on he was too heavy," Scott recalled.

British military records show that Duffy died on April 23, 1915, from his wounds in a Canadian field ambulance. In his absence, Fabre had finally won the Boston Marathon four days earlier.

MEMORIES STILL HAUNT BOTH SIDES OF THE GALLIPOLI TRAGEDY

Gallipoli, Turkey

WHENEVER HE LEAVES THE HOUSE, Kenan Ersoz hides the bayonet his father used to defend the crumbling Ottoman Empire against the British-led invasion of Gallipoli a century ago. The father saw it as a friend that kept him alive. The son keeps it as his most prized possession.

The 1915 campaign is no less present for descendants of soldiers from Australia and New Zealand who played a leading role for the other side.

John Carnell traveled from Sydney with his wife, Carol, and two children, Kate and Tom, to visit spots where his great-grandfather landed on the peninsula—and where he was mortally wounded months later.

"People only really die when the living stop talking about them," he said. "I can bang on about my ancestor for another 20 years or so. My children can do it for 50 and they can tell their grandchildren."

As world leaders gathered in 2015 with the descendants, the memories of one of the most harrowing campaigns of the 20th century have come surging back to life. The doomed Allied offensive to secure a naval route from the Mediterranean to Istanbul through the Dardanelles, and take the Ottomans out of the war, resulted in over 130,000 deaths on both sides. It came to be seen as a folly of British war planning.

The campaign's enduring poignancy may be that it forged national identities for countries on both sides.

Mustafa Kemal Ataturk used his prominence as a commander at Gallipoli, known as Canakkale to the Turks, to vault into prominence, lead Turkey's War of Independence—and ultimately found the Turkish Republic. Similarly, the tragic fate of troops from Australia and New Zealand, who played a key role in the campaign, is said to have inspired an identity distinct from Britain. The anniversary of the start of the land campaign on April 25, known as ANZAC Day, after the Australia and New Zealand Army Corps, is marked as a coming of age for both nations.

Carnell's great-grandfather, Francis George Carnell, was so eager he had to lie about his age. That was a common ploy for teenagers of the day. But Francis was 55—and too old to enlist. He had already fought in wars in South Africa for the British. After being promoted to lance corporal in training, he landed at what is now known as Anzac cove among the early waves of soldiers.

On April 25, 1915, they were rowed in at dawn to narrow beaches with scant cover only to encounter rugged hills and scorching fire by well concealed Turkish defenders.

John Carnell knows little about what happened next, except that somehow his ancestor, despite his age, made it up the beach to fight in one of the iconic battles of the campaign. The fight for the Turkish position of "Lone Pine"—launched by Australian battalions—cost heavy losses on both sides. On Saturday, Australians will commemorate that battle following a dawn service at Anzac Cove, near a memorial with the names of dead soldiers, including. F.G. Carnell.

Memories Still Haunt Both Sides of the Gallipoli Tragedy

On Aug. 7, Francis George Carnell was wounded and evacuated to a hospital ship. He died on Aug. 10, according to John Carnell, and was buried at sea. He left behind a wife and one son, who had thirteen children.

That same summer, Mehmet Emin Ersoz—Kenan's father—was also gravely injured. The father talked little of the war, and Kenan thinks it was because he wanted to spare the children his suffering.

But there was no hiding it.

"We could see the ugly side of war on my father's body," he said. "His feet were full of wounds. There were callused pieces between his flesh and bones."

His father carried shrapnel in his head until he died in 1970. Kenan was told his father was wounded "when the grapes on the peninsula were ripe"—placing it in August or early September.

Mehmet Emin Ersoz was proud to keep his bayonet close-by until death. But he regretted having to carry the enemy's metal with him, too.

"That was the one thing that saddened him most," Kenan Ersoz said.

Ersoz said nothing good came from the battles except Turkey's defense: "War, as it has long been, consists of blood, gunpowder, pain, tears."

John Carnell sees a more positive message—one that comes from the onetime enemy.

On Australian flags embroidered with his ancestor's records, there's also a quote from Ataturk that pays tribute to the fallen from Australia and New Zealand:

"You are now lying in the soil of a friendly country. Therefore rest in peace. There is no difference between the Johnnies and the Mehmets to us," the eulogy reads. "They have become our sons as well."

ALAN SEEGER, POET-SOLDIER, WHO FOUGHT AS AN AMERICAN WITH FRANCE IN WORLD WAR I

Belloy-en Santerre, France

IN THE END, ALAN SEEGER'S BONES could no longer be distinguished from those of his Foreign Legion comrades who had fallen alongside him in one of the most brutal battles of World War I.

United across nations, it was the glorious death that he craved.

Seeger — an American poet, romantic and soldier — died on that most American of days, July 4th. The year was 1916. Barely 28, he was already fighting for a global, common cause that bound dozens of countries together at a time when the United States was still a bystander, reluctant to get involved in a faraway war in Europe.

His premonition, "I have a Rendezvous with Death," was to become his most beloved poem, and the volunteer was happy to give his life for France and its grand ideals of "Liberty, Equality and Fraternity." Half a century later, it was a favorite poem of U.S. President John Kennedy. And French

President Emmanuel Macron referred to him in a speech to Congress in April, 2018 to highlight the tight bonds of Franco-American friendship.

Seeger was last seen by his Egyptian friend Rif Baer charging the German enemy—a tiny part of the massive Battle of the Somme, where more than 1 million people were killed, wounded or went missing in 4½ months of fighting in 1916.

"His head erect, and pride in his eye, I saw him running forward, with bayonet fixed. Soon he disappeared," Baer described the final scene—and the myth of Seeger emerged.

On a summer's day, peonies bloomed over Ossuary No. 1 in nearby Lihons where he is believed to lie, forgotten by most but still cherished by some. In the village where he fell, a gnarly apple tree planted in dedication to his sacrifice furtively tried to produce fruit from the few branches it still has.

The Belloy village square is named after him and the village's World War I memorial even has him—in the Gallic "Alain Seeger" -chiseled in stone.

"For France, Alan Seeger is first and foremost the symbol of commitment—commitment right up to death," said local historian Marcel Queyrat.

In his diary, Seeger wrote "I never took arms out of any hatred against Germany or the Germans, but purely out of love for France."

To his mother he wrote "there should really be no neutrals in a conflict like this, where there is not a people whose interests are not involved." This, combined with his French military flair for "elan"—the forward thrust in battle—makes Seeger a standout a century later when Europeans are questioning whether the United States under President Trump still feels a sense of trans-Atlantic unity.

From the start of World War I, Seeger wanted to get the United States involved in the allied cause. Once it did, in 1917, it set the scene for the "American century" of predominance in the world.

Seeger could not understand those who stood to the side in World War I, hardly the anti-war message that his folk-singing nephew Pete Seeger would later spread during the Vietnam War years.

"Playing a part in the life of nations, he is taking part in the largest movement his planet allows him," Alan Seeger wrote in his diary.

Born into a wealthy family that built its fortune on Mexican sugar refining, and with a gift for languages, he went to study at Harvard. His life changed for good when he started hanging out with classmate John Reed, who went on to become the eyewitness writer of the 1917 Russian Communist revolution with "Ten Days that Shook the World."

After Harvard, it was on to New York and the Bohemian lifestyle of Greenwich Village. Soon Seeger was crossing the Atlantic to Paris and the Rive Gauche—the Left Bank. He arrived there in 1912, giving him two years to fall in love with the City of Lights and all things French, enough to decide to defend the nation when war came.

"An artist is not only an artist, he is also a man of action which, for me, is absolutely essential," said Pierre-Emmanuel Taittinger, president of the famed family Champagne house. "Seeger shows the way."

Taittinger has been smitten with Seeger's dash. At his Chateau de la Marquetterie amid the Champagne vineyards, he even has a special room with poetry and photos of Seeger, amid other World War I memorabilia. Seeger was smitten just as much with Champagne, writing of a night when he and other soldiers "in our candle-lit loft we uncorked bottles of bubbling champagne . . . and clinking our tin army cups."

Early on, there was much fighting around Reims, Champagne's main city, and the destruction of the Cathedral by the Germans was considered such a sacrilege that it turned many across the world against Kaiser Wilhelm II. Those were the fields amid vines that soldier Seeger roamed early on—often behind the lines while his soul yearned for action.

"And what a curious anomaly," he wrote to his mother. "On this slope the grape pickers are singing merrily at their work, on the other the batteries are roaming. Boom! Boom!"

Even though France was in his heart, home kept tugging at it too. He "fairly danced for joy" being granted a July 4th leave in Paris in 1915, but the war malaise had already spread to the capital, where Seeger saw many women in mourning. It was to be his last full Independence Day.

With an uncanny sense of fate, he felt battle was near in June 1916. "We will go directly into action, magnificently, unexpectedly, and probably victoriously, in some dashing charge, even if it be only of local importance," he wrote.

That is exactly what happened at Belloy-en-Santerre.

"I have a rendezvous with Death—At some disputed barricade," the poem says.

That is how Seeger is remembered.

"Life is very short but some lives are more full than others," said the 63-year-old Taittinger, adding that Seeger's life, cut short at 28, "is much more full than my life will ever be."

THE UNITED STATES JOINED WORLD WAR I TO MAKE THE DIFFERENCE

Romagne-Sous-Montfaucon, France

CARPENTER GUY FORD LIKED TO WATCH fish play in the currents around his ship as it sailed for Europe to offload untested troops for a war as horrendous as it was defining for the century to come.

Ford would soon lose his innocence. But unlike many young Americans who crossed the Atlantic a century ago to fight in World War I, he lived to see his country go from a fledging, inward-looking nation to a world power.

Before April 6, 1917, the United States still was, in the words of American writer Walter Lippmann, a country where "money spent on battleships would be better spent on schoolhouses."

The United States Joined World War I to Make the Difference

Then, the United States declared war on Germany and, following victory in 1918, started what would eventually become known as "The American Century."

AMERICA FIRST

Guy Ford, an only child from Ronceverte, West Virginia, was closing in on 30 when the so-called Great War started in August 1914. Two months earlier, a Serb nationalist named Gavrilo Princip had shot and killed Austro-Hungarian Crown Prince Franz Ferdinand in Sarajevo.

The shot was heard around Europe, where diplomatic alliances quickly drew most of the continent into war, with Germany and the Austro-Hungarian Empire pitted against Britain, Russia and France. But the reverberations didn't immediately cross the Atlantic.

"The attitude of the Americans was not yet the attitude of a big power," said Professor Luc De Vos, a military historian of Leuven University.

American immigrant communities were torn over whether to help the British, and pacifism was the watchword after the destruction of the U.S. Civil War. President Woodrow Wilson won re-election in 1916 with the slogan "He has kept us out of war." Another of his campaign catchphrases had a more contemporary ring: "America first."

In Europe, both sides had already dug in for trench warfare in northern France and Belgium, with gas and tanks and precision shelling making battle more deadly than ever. Some days there were tens of thousands of casualties in unprecedented slaughter.

Ford's granddaughter, Mary Thompson, who also lives in West Virginia, retraced his steps through the war and stopped off at Verdun in northern France. There, the mangled remains of some 130,000 unknown soldiers from both sides, impossible to separate, lie together in the Douaumont Ossuary.

"I can't imagine a boy from Summers County in West Virginia coming to this country and marching ahead of death bombs," she said.

Nor, for most of the war, could most Americans.

IT HAS STIRRED US VERY DEEPLY

Despite American reluctance to get involved, there was outrage early on at the bombing and German destruction of Belgium's Louvain library and reports of other atrocities. Then, German submarines started attacking ships in the Atlantic. In 1915, the British liner Lusitania was torpedoed, killing some 1,200, including 128 Americans. Early in 1917, unrestricted submarine warfare resumed. In his April 2 war message to Congress, Wilson called it "warfare against mankind."

"American ships have been sunk, American lives taken, in ways which it has stirred us very deeply to learn of," he said, four days before war was declared.

And in a diplomatic faux pas with huge consequences, German Foreign Minister Arthur Zimmermann sent a telegram to his Mexico City office to draw Mexico into the war with a promise to get territory back in Texas, New Mexico and Arizona. There was no WikiLeaks then, but British intelligence got hold of the missive and fed it to Wilson.

"It means to stir up enemies against us at our very doors," Wilson said.

He asked for war. On April 6, Congress obliged.

THEY WERE ESSENTIAL

By then, millions had already died. The U.S. entry changed everything.

"Yes, they were essential in turning the tide. Why? There was a real deadlock," said De Vos, the historian. Tens of thousands of lives were wasted as one side advanced a few miles (kilometers) on the Western Front, from one trench to the other, and then back. "The big problem was: how to break through the front?"

It took more than a year for Guy Ford and hundreds of thousands of other young Americans to be ready for the front lines.

When war was declared, "the U.S. army was smaller than the Danish army and much smaller than the Belgian army," De Vos said.

The British and French wanted them fast, but commander Gen. John J. Pershing insisted his troops needed training first.

So it was May 26, 1918, before Ford, drafted by the American Expeditionary Force, left for France. He kept a small diary noting in short form how seas were rough, target practice was held and with "wind blowing schools of fish at play."

He landed in Brest, France's westernmost port on the tip of Brittany, on June 8. On Independence Day that July 4, when others at home would have been celebrating and drinking, his entry in the diary consisted of "Left Halinghen, hiked to Samer. Loaded on train. That night was issued overcoat before leaving. Air raid that night."

As he was making the 850-kilometer (530-mile) trip across France to the Verdun region with the 305th Engineering Battalion of the 80th Division, the war was entering its end game, the outcome much more uncertain than it seems now in hindsight.

Germany had long fought on two fronts, against Russia in the east and France and Belgium in the west. When Russia signed a peace treaty in 1918, Germany was able to pull troops west and push for the decisive breakthrough. The Germans came within bombardment reach of Paris, but failed again to fully turn the war.

From then on, the arrival of up to 2.1 million U.S. troops became an ever-bigger factor.

"At that decisive moment in the balance of powers, the 2 million Americans—young, enthusiastic troops, they attacked and they were everywhere on the front," De Vos said.

The sense of urgency and stress of battle was evident in Ford's diary, where verbs were in increasingly short supply, giving way to the staccato rendering of villages and dates—ever closer to the America's defining World War I battle of Meuse-Argonne, a region in eastern France close to Verdun.

THE DEAD MAN

A century later, little has changed in the landscape of the Meuse-Argonne where Ford fought, with neat patches of rich pasture cutting a line between opposing forests that once provided a hiding place for the American and German soldiers behind the lines.

At a vital stage of World War I in the fall of 1918, the Meuse-Argonne offensive was the biggest and bloodiest operation of the American Expeditionary Force. It involved more than 1.2 million American soldiers and lasted 47 days, with a loss of over 26,000 American lives. Ford survived.

Today, only chirping birds and the distant hum of lawnmowers break the solemn silence at the vast estate of the Meuse-Argonne American Cemetery in Romagne-Sous-Montfaucon. It is the largest American cemetery in Europe and memorializes 15,200 war dead. The stark white crosses, lined up in neat rows between the trees, are engraved with each soldier's name, rank, home state and date of death.

"I'm moved to tears," said Mary Thompson's husband, Bob. "It brings it all home. I know these towns and states. I almost feel like I know these people."

At huge cost, the Americans were driving the Germans back ever farther when, on Nov. 11, the armistice ended the fighting.

Ford wrote only "Nov. 11—Hiked to Le Mort-Hommes," a slight misspelling of the ghost village aptly named The Dead Man. The reports of a spontaneous concert, bonfires and massive rejoicing at the momentous victory within the regiment never made it into his diary. Emotion was dulled to the extent that for the next day, he wrote only "12—to Chatel."

Some never made it that far. Even a century later, a day could make a fateful difference. One white marble headstone at Meuse-Argonne reads "ROGERS E. TRAHAN SERGT. 9 INF. 2 DIV. LOUISIANA NOV 11, 1918."

IT COULD HAVE BEEN SOMETHING FROM THE WAR

In May of 1919, Guy Ford returned to life in West Virginia, officially authorized by the 305th engineers "to wear the Service Ribbon" with three bronze stars, for having participated in the Somme, St. Mihiel and Meuse-Argonne offensives.

As much of Europe lay in ruins, with 14 million soldiers and civilians from around the globe dead, the United States emerged as a major power in the world.

In "a personal word" to his soldiers in which he signed off as commander in chief, Gen. Pershing wrote that they "in a succession of brilliant offensives have overcome the menace to our civilization."

Ford eventually married and had a boy and then a set of twin boys. In 1934, when Mary Thompson's father was just four, Ford died at the age of 46. Countless people had returned from the war with physical and mental scars never fully examined.

"We'll never know what caused his death," Mary Thompson said. "We understood from relatives that it was his heart, but who knows—it could have been something from the war."

INNOVATIONS A CENTURY AGO, BUT STILL WITH US

London, England

MACHINE GUNS. TANKS. CHEMICAL WEAPONS. Warplanes. Submarines. Trench coats. Wristwatches. Some of the innovations that were developed or came into wide use during World War I are still with us today.

The world's first mechanized war introduced enhanced weaponry and equipment, most of it designed to take lives but some of it aimed at saving lives. A look at some of the things that were new a century ago that we take for granted today:

MACHINE GUNS

Hand-cranked, high-capacity, rapid-firing firearms had been used as far back as the Civil War. But it was American inventor Hiram Maxim's 1880s design for a single-barrel, portable machine gun and other later versions that became ubiquitous on both sides during World War I. It forced opposing forces to dig hundreds of miles of trenches, with a deadly "no man's land" in between where soldiers could get mowed down.

This kind of fighting was unfamiliar to most American forces, who had been trained in the tactics of mobile warfare, always advancing. "Then it becomes, 'How do we get out of the trenches?'" said Maj. Kyle Hatzinger, a history instructor at the U.S. Military Academy at West Point. "The Americans by 1917 have to figure this out."

TANKS

One way to break out of the trenches along the Western Front was to bust through with newly developed armored tracked vehicles dubbed tanks. The British introduced a large number of tanks to the battlefield for the first time in September 1916, during the battle of the Somme. Other armies soon were developing their own versions. In September 1918, a 32-year-old Army lieutenant colonel named George Patton led a U.S. tank unit into battle for the first time. A quarter century later, during World War II, he was the most famous commander of American armored units.

CHEMICAL WEAPONS

Germany launched the first use of a chemical weapon, chlorine gas, at Ypres, Belgium, in April 1915, against French troops. By 1917 other chemicals, including mustard gas, were being used by both sides. Some estimates put the number of deaths from gas attacks at about 900,000, with another 1 million injured. Gas masks were developed. But using gas could result in friendly fire casualties when winds blew the toxic fumes back into the attackers' positions.

"And if you attack you now have to go through the gas cloud you've created," Hatzinger said. "There's a lot of trial and error with the technology."

Outrage over the use of chemicals weapons in WWI led to the 1925 Geneva Protocol treaty that banned the use of chemical or biological weapons in international armed conflicts.

AIR WARFARE

A little more than a decade after the Wright Brothers flew their first airplane, WWI combatants took to the skies to spy on one another—and then to shoot each other down. Early in the war, aircraft were equipped with cameras for taking reconnaissance photographs. Pilots started arming themselves with handguns and rifles to shoot down enemy biplanes. Soon, mounted machine guns were being used in aerial combat known as dogfights, giving rise to such legendary fighter aces as Germany's Manfred von Richthofen (aka 'The Red Baron'), American Eddie Rickenbacker and Canada's Billy Bishop.

SUBMARINES

Using submersible vessels to attack enemy ships had been tried as far back as the American Revolution. It wasn't until WWI that submarines were used in large numbers as part of naval operations. Germany was the first nation to fully utilize submarine technology, attacking Allied shipping in the Atlantic and infamously sinking the British ocean liner RMS Lusitania off the Irish coast in May 1915, killing 1,200 people, including 128 Americans. The outcry from the U.S. over the attack prompted Germany to shift much of its submarine attacks elsewhere. But the Germans resumed submarine attacks in early 1917 and sank several U.S. vessels, one of the key reasons for America entering the war.

BARBED WIRE

Invented in post-Civil War America for Midwestern homesteaders to confine their livestock, the strands of twisted wire with sharpened spurs could also be used to keep soldiers from reaching an enemy's positions. During WWI it was placed in front of trenches or arranged in such a way that enemy ground assaults were funneled into areas covered by machine gun and artillery fire. Barbed wire fences were ubiquitous on the Western Front, where snared soldiers made easy targets for small-arms fire.

PORTABLE X-RAYS

Radiology pioneer Marie Curie is credited with coming up with the idea of loading X-ray machines onto vehicles and driving to the front lines outside

World War I

Paris to treat wounded French soldiers. The fleet of modified vehicles she assembled served as mobile X-ray units that were credited with saving thousands of lives. Today's military medical support units can take the high-tech versions as close to the fighting as possible to examine wounded soldiers before sending them to larger field hospitals.

TRENCH COATS AND WRISTWATCHES

They weren't fashion accessories.

Trench coats replaced the earlier era's full-length, woolen great coats, which became heavy when wet. British officers serving in the trenches turned to established English clothing firms such as Burberry and Aquascutum for khaki-colored, waterproof coats with deep pockets large enough to hold maps and a belt at the waist with metal D-rings for attaching gear.

Wristwatches had been around in some form for decades, mostly as jewelry worn by women, but they became standard equipment for soldiers and pilots who didn't want to be fumbling for the traditional pocket watch while launching artillery-supported ground assaults or flying combat missions.

WOMEN IN UNIFORM

WWI was the first time in the nation's history that women were officially attached to branches of the U.S. military, and more than 30,000 served in uniform, mostly as nurses or switchboard operators. Thousands of other women joined the various stateside private organizations aiding the war effort, and they also wore uniforms.

A cartoon in popular Life magazine at the time showed two American soldiers looking at a young woman working at a desk job. "What will you do after the war if you can't get your old job back?" one asked. The other replied: "Marry the girl who's holding it down."

PATRIOTIC PROPAGANDA

American James Montgomery Flagg created the now-famous poster of a pointing Uncle Sam under the words "I Want You." Some 4 million copies of the U.S. version of the Army recruitment poster were printed in 1917-18, according to the Library of Congress website. The poster proved so popular it was re-introduced during World War II, when millions more were printed.

Similarly popular was George M. Cohan's jaunty wartime ditty "Over There," which proudly spread word to Europe that "the Yanks are coming." More than 2 million copies of the song's sheet music were sold by the end of the war.

VIMY — THE WORLD WAR I BATTLE THAT DEFINED CANADA

Vimy, France

AN OCEAN AWAY FROM HOME, spilling their blood on a remote ridge in the muddied battlefields of northern France a century ago, many would argue that Canadians earned the right to become a nation here.

Vimy Ridge has become much more than a speck on a French map, even much more than a famous World War I battle. In a fledgling nation looking for a sense of self, trying to set it apart from British rule, the battle provided everything it needed—the vision of an underdog beating the odds, a show of courage, resolve and unity.

"In this sense, Canada was born there," Prime Minister Justin Trudeau said in April, 2017 during the centennial of the battle amid the fertile countryside of northern France, where any hill with a view was fought over with a blind determination costing thousands of lives in World War I.

Canada lost 3,600 soldiers and had over 7,000 injured during the four-day battle.

"They were, most of them, young men in their late teens, in their early 20s," Trudeau said. "Going as far as sacrificing their lives, these men both ordinary and extraordinary of the British dominion fought for the first time as citizens of a single and same country . . . side by side here in Vimy." Historians agree. "It made the Canadian Corps think it could do anything. It made the soldiers believe that they were really good soldiers, better than anybody else. They had done something that the British and French were not able to do," said Professor Jack Granatstein, a Canadian military historian.

British and French forces had tried for a long time but failed to take Vimy Ridge. The Canadians succeeded on April 9, 1917, battling through snow and sleet to push out the Germans, who had long held the strategic post.

In the grand scheme of the war, it amounted to little.

"It did not win the war. It did not change the course of the war. It moved the Germans back several kilometers, but that was it," Granatstein said.

For Canada though, it meant everything.

"In one day — in fact in one morning — these civilian volunteers from a small country with no military tradition were expected to do what the British and French had failed to do in two years," Pierre Berton wrote in his 1985 book, "Vimy."

It would take more than a year to finally budge the front line and start pushing the Germans back. The Canadians, ever more emboldened after Vimy, played their part and even were among the signatories to the Versailles Treaty.

Among the string of war monuments reaching from the North Sea to Switzerland, Vimy stands out as perhaps the finest.

With its surging pale columns reaching skyward, it stirs the soul. Yet statues of the Weeping Woman and two mourners, and the list of 11,285 soldiers posted "missing, presumed dead," makes it a solemn pilgrimage site.

The Vimy memorial, a revered national symbol, is on the back of Canada's $20 bill to this day.

SPY, TEMPTRESS, VICTIM? MATA HARI STILL ELUDES DEFINITION

Leeuwarden, Netherlands

HER LIFE AND DEATH BECAME fodder almost overnight for one of the greatest spy stories of all time—featuring an alluring temptress who could dance, dazzle and draw secrets from the hapless military men unable to resist her.

A century ago, an exotic dancer named Mata Hari was executed by a French firing squad, condemned as a sultry Dutch double agent who supposedly caused the deaths of thousands of soldiers during World War I.

Increasingly, though, Mata Hari—the stage name adopted by Margaretha Zelle—is also being reinterpreted as a victim of a time when a sexually liberated woman with artistic ambitions faced harsh judgment.

The irony is not missed on Yves Rocourt, curator of "Mata Hari. The Myth and the Maiden," a 2017 exhibit in Leeuwarden, the Dutch town where Zelle was born in 1876.

"Unfortunately, issues like money and having to sleep with someone in a position of power to achieve something are not time-related," Rocourt said.

"You cannot help but think about what is going in Hollywood at this very moment," said Julie Wheelwright, author of the biography "The Fatal Lover." "All these allegations that are coming out now and you just wonder, 'But what's changed in 100 years?' Not much."

On a canal close to her childhood home, where vicious winds and icy temperatures can freeze the water for months, a statue erected in 1976 shows Mata Hari in her typical stage regalia. Dressed in little more than pearls and veils, she stands with legs apart and arms outstretched, ready to take on the world.

How she got to the glittering salons and theaters of Paris and Berlin before ending up in front of a firing squad was due to desperation as much as boldness.

Her comfortable youth was disrupted when her father went broke and her mother died. At age 18, she answered an ad placed by an aristocrat military officer seeking a wife. Soon, she was living in the Dutch East Indies, in what is now Indonesia.

The couple had two children despite her husband's violence and unfaithfulness and Margaretha's own fiery, flirtatious personality. After their son died, the marriage disintegrated and her ex-husband refused to pay alimony. Zelle, facing being a single mother without financial support, gave up custody of her daughter and in 1903 left for Paris, where she reinvented herself.

"I am tired of struggling against life," she wrote. The choice she saw was to "be a decent mother or live life as it is dazzlingly offered to me here."

Lourens Oldersma, who edited a book of Mata Hari's letters, said "she evolved from being a flirt into the woman that started living this loose, decadent life."

Building a dance repertoire on the sensuous temple dances she had observed in Asia, Mata Hari had her breakthrough performance at the

Paris Musee Guimet on March 13, 1905. She soon became a sensation across Europe.

But the brilliant life she envisioned was expensive to maintain, especially as she got older and her popularity as an exotic dancer declined. When World War I broke out, she used her passport from a neutral country to continue traveling and took wealthy, well-connected lovers from all sides of the conflict.

The promise of a steady supply of francs to support herself persuaded Zelle to accept an offer to spy, first for Germany and then for France.

"She thought that spying was just another role. It was another kind of performance," Wheelwright said. "She was very naive."

French intelligence eventually intercepted a German telegram discussing the work of an agent codenamed H-21. The details revealed Mata Hari as a double agent two-timing France. She was arrested while having breakfast in her suite at the Elysee Palace Hotel.

During 16 interrogation sessions, she cracked and admitted to working for the Germans. At 41, she was shot at a military ground close to Paris at dawn on Oct. 15, 1917.

The rest is history—and an awful lot of books and movies, including one starring Greta Garbo. Mata Hari's story ebbs and flows with the mood of the times and geography.

"When I was talking to people in France, even until quite recently, their view was very much more that 'Here was this decadent woman who was responsible for all these deaths, so why should we feel any sympathy for her?'" Wheelwright said.

In the Netherlands, there was more ambivalence.

"They stressed more the spy story and the exotic dancer rather than the fact she was a decadent woman," Oldersma said.

With the publication of his book last year, "people started realizing that, yes, this is also a mother, and she had to go through a fight," he said.

Still, the question of who Mata Hari really was defies easy answers. One year she refused to pose naked for a painter, the next she slept with men for money. The verdict on whether the secrets she gained from her lovers' lips doomed thousands of young Allied soldiers continues to be debated but seems increasingly unlikely.

"There is a kind of paradoxical thing going on," Wheelwright said. "On the one hand, she is very vulnerable. But then on the other hand, she's also got a sense of manipulating people."

The mystery of Mata Hari still confounds Rocourt, the exhibit curator. "The truth is very complex," he said. "I don't know what the truth is."

ONE VICTOROUS BATTLE THAT BECAME A DEFINING MOMENT FOR THE UNITED STATES

Belleau, France

IT WAS THE SPRING OF 1918, and the German army was making a final push toward Paris. The only thing in their way was a contingent of Allied troops, including untested U.S. forces near the Marne River in northern France.

Among them: U.S. Army 1st Lt. Gordon Kaemmerling, a precocious and athletic Harvard graduate who had jumped at the opportunity to help the United States leave its shell of isolationism and join the war.

On June 6, 1918, the U.S. forces attacked, storming across the open

One Victorous Battle that Became a Defining Moment for the United States

fields near Belleau Wood. Germans sprayed them with shells and machine-gun fire from a densely forested hill. Without proper artillery cover, the Americans were mowed down easily at first.

In the chaos, the 26-year-old Kaemmerling rushed to help his comrades, and was nearly torn in two by shrapnel and bullets.

The bravery of Kaemmerling and others helped the Americans chase the German forces out of Belleau Wood by the end of the month. The battle became a defining moment in World War I, not just containing the German push along the Western Front but proving the Americans' military mettle for all to see.

Victory bonded the Allies, and that friendship became the cornerstone of global diplomacy for most of the last 100 years.

NO RETREAT

Germany acknowledged the arrival of the U.S. forces on the Western Front would be a burden, but peace with the Bolsheviks in Soviet Russia meant that German troops could reinforce another onslaught on France.

It was a unique window of opportunity for the Germans, and when it came, they got within a week's march from Paris. Victory after four years of fighting seemed possible.

The American force "was still considered a very untried organization, and among the French and British, they were not sure how well they would perform," said retired U.S. Army Col. David S. Jones, a historian.

The initial plan was to give many of the U.S. forces more time to train before being thrown into battle, but Germany had other ideas.

In desperation, the French asked U.S. Gen. John J. "Black Jack" Pershing for the immediate deployment of his some of his troops to stop the gap near the Marne, northeast of Paris. U.S. soldiers and Marines were soon sent off to Belleau.

The combination of inexperience and gung-ho enthusiasm became the stuff of legend. The battle is one of the first things taught to any U.S. Marine, said Owen Gardner Finnegan, a Marine who served in Afghanistan and was visiting the Belleau Wood cemetery.

Because of their ferocity, the Americans "stopped the most advanced army in the world at the time in savage fighting," Finnegan said.

Marine Corps lore has it that one officer, told there was a general retreat, said, "Retreat? Hell, we just got here!"

The Americans made their vigor, youth and resilience count against the more experienced but battle-weary Germans, who were approaching their fifth year of fighting.

When the Americans were confronted with "intense enemy fire, instead of ducking, instead of retreating, they charged," said French historian Jean-Michel Steg.

At first, it was a matter of survival. Steadily, however, they established themselves in hostile terrain where any tree could hide an enemy. They stood their ground in man-to-man fighting.

Instead of marching on Paris, the Germans soon found themselves on the back foot.

Much more was at stake than a patch of ground along a 350-mile (560-kilometer) front line.

"It became something different. It became a test of will," Steg said.

Bolstered by the Americans, the Allies were pushing the Germans back.

"The turning point was that the Germans came to the realization that the American Army was for real and was not only going to get bigger with the arrival of new soldiers each month but was also going to get better," Steg said.

By the end of 1918, more than 2 million Americans were on the front.

Belleau Wood "definitely was a critical point in the road for America becoming a world power," Jones said.

Other successes by U.S., French and British Commonwealth forces led to the armistice of Nov. 11, 1918.

The U.S. would return again to Europe to fight and defeat the Germans in World War II. It spread its global reach to embody what some have called the "American Century."

A SYMBOLIC TREE

A century after the battle, shell holes are covered in fir and ivy, and there are enough oak saplings in Belleau Wood that some escape the appetite of roving deer.

One Victorous Battle that Became a Defining Moment for the United States

One young tree was dug up for a special purpose: On a state visit in April 2018, French President Emmanuel Macron brought it to the White House for a replanting ceremony with President Donald Trump.

Macron said the tree could take root "as a symbol of the sacrifice and the common battles that France and the United States have led together."

Although Macron and Trump celebrated that bond, there were many strains between the U.S. and Europe—on climate change, the Iran nuclear deal, relations with Russia and trans-Atlantic trade.

That spring, European Union President Donald Tusk, referring to the Trump administration, said: "Someone could even think, 'with friends like that, who needs enemies?'"

It was not a sentiment that Owen Gardner Finnegan, the Marine who was visiting Belleau Wood, wanted to dwell on as he stood among the white marble grave markers of the fallen Americans on a gray spring day.

"We should remember all of this—the verdant green fields of France that were stained with the blood of several million men," Finnegan said.

In a letter home, Gordon Kaemmerling described France as "a dream country that I'd love to play in in peace times."

He never got the chance. He was buried in the Ainse-Marne American Cemetery in Belleau, one of 2,289 Americans laid to rest there.

"He was a leader of men, and in order to lead, he needed to be out front," said Shane Williams, the cemetery's superintendent.

WORLD WAR I MUNITIONS STILL MAKING THEIR WAY ONTO THE BEACHES AN OCEAN AWAY

Mantoloking, NJ, USA

A CENTURY AFTER WORLD WAR I ended, discarded munitions from that and other wars continue to make their way onto beaches around the country.

Items ranging from tiny fuses to full-scale mines are displaced by beach replenishment projects, sucked from the ocean floor and pumped ashore, or by strong storms that uncover them.

A recent discovery came in early 2018 when seven WWI rifle grenades were found on the beach in Mantoloking, New Jersey, which is undergoing a beach replenishment project to undo damage from Superstorm Sandy more than five years ago.

World War I Munitions Still Making Their Way Onto the Beaches an Ocean Away

Many of the items were simply dumped overboard at the end of World Wars I and II; others remain from military drills or target practice. They've been discovered in at least 16 states from New Jersey to Hawaii.

"Surprisingly or not, this stuff continues to turn up," said Niall Slowey, an oceanography professor at Texas A&M University, who has studied the phenomenon extensively. "They disposed of millions of tons of this stuff."

No one knows how many pieces of munitions remain offshore, partly because the military's own records as to how much was disposed of aren't great. A Defense Department report to Congress in 2009 said more than half of sea disposals of munitions was done in the Atlantic Ocean; the Pacific got another 35 percent, and lesser amounts were dumped off Hawaii, Alaska, the Gulf of Mexico and the Caribbean. The material was dumped as near as 5 miles from shore, in water as shallow as 50 feet.

Slowey and a colleague released a 2012 study estimating there are millions of pounds of undersea bombs in the Gulf of Mexico alone.

Disposal of unneeded munitions at sea was commonly accepted practice until 1970.

"They thought it was beyond harm's reach," Slowey said. "People could not envision that there would be any interaction with material that deep on the ocean floor. But there is a lot more on the sea floor than anyone could have envisioned."

New Jersey has been home to some well-publicized discoveries, including more than 1,100 pieces of munitions pumped ashore during beach replenishment work on a mile and a half of sand in Surf City and Ship Bottom on Long Beach Island in 2007. The items, mostly fuses, prompted temporary bans on the use of metal detectors and the digging of holes in the sand more than a foot deep. It also created a cottage industry in T-shirts with slogans like "Our beaches will blow you away!" and "I got bombed on L.B.I.!"

Similar material surfaced on the Jersey shore towns of Loch Arbour, Allenhurst and Deal in 2016 as part of another post-Sandy beach restoration project.

In May 2008, a bomb squad from the Massachusetts State Police detonated several pieces of unexploded ordnance left over from World War II on Chappaquiddick, including practice bombs.

In June 2013, a beachgoer discovered a partially buried German mine in the surf about 10 feet from shore in Bay Head, New Jersey, on the same day that the Assateague Island National Seashore in Maryland did a controlled explosion of a World War II bomb that had washed ashore.

In July 2015, a photoflash bomb, designed to illuminate the night sky over WWII battlefields, was discovered on a beach near Tampa, Florida, where authorities blew it up on the sand.

Military and civilian experts say they don't know of anyone in the United States being injured by munitions found on a beach, but agree the potential for injury is real.

"The problem is you just don't know," said Master Sgt. Brad Kline, an explosives disposal expert at New Jersey's Joint Base McGuire-Dix-Lakehurst. "There could be explosive residue left behind. It's definitely not worth the risk" of handling it. Military personnel use explosives to blow up munitions that are discovered on the beach and brought to the base.

In Europe, there have been injuries and deaths from unexploded munitions, including the 2005 deaths of three Dutch fishermen whose nets brought a WWII bomb to the surface, and other fishermen burned by chemical weapons they unwittingly dredged up.

ONE LONE SUBMARINE BROUGHT WORLD WAR I HOME TO THE UNITED STATES

Orleans, MA, USA

OVER 3,000 MILES FROM THE TRENCHES and battlefields of the Western Front, where many hundreds of thousands had already died, residents of Orleans, Massachusetts, were enjoying a typical summer morning on July 21, 1918, waiting for the fog to lift off the shore.

Then suddenly, a German U-156 submarine broke the surface and brought World War I home. Orleans became the only part of the United States to be shelled by the enemy. For a brief moment, "over there" had become "over here."

Just after 10.30 a.m., the heavy thump of something hitting land signaled the first attack on American soil in 100 years.

"I don't know if it was the first shot or the sound of my feet hitting the floor," the late Ruben Hopkins, then a 22-year-old guard at Orleans' lifesaving station No. 40, recalled in a recording. "I was out of my bunk up there in seconds flat."

To this day, it remains a mystery why such an advanced submarine would attack a target that had no real value. While instilling fear in the American public by attacking shipping was a tactic, going so close to shore seemed an undue risk. One theory is that the sub had hoped to cut the underwater communications cable that ran from Orleans to France.

That day, the Perth Amboy tug, towing four barges, was taking the long route around the elbow of Cape Cod rather than passing through the newly opened Cape Cod Canal. German Capt. Richard Feldt's U-156 was watching and started shooting.

Looking out from the station watchtower window, Hopkins recalled: "I could clearly make out the shape of the submarine. I saw a splash where it hit in the water next to the tug."

The Perth Amboy took a direct hit to the pilothouse, and a member of the crew was wounded. The sub then directed its attention to the barges.

The local lifesavers, some of the best in the U.S., launched their boat directly into the line of fire. Their motto: "You have to go out, but you don't have to come back." Nothing, however, really prepared the lifesavers for such a close encounter with the enemy.

Residents flocked to the beach to see what the excitement was about before shells hitting land sent some scurrying back home. Dr. Danforth Taylor, visiting his daughter on the bluff above Nauset Beach, telephoned The Boston Globe immediately.

Miles away at the Chatham Naval Air Station, Ensign Eric Lingard piloted an HS-1L flying boat and flew north, since lifesavers had already reached the tug and barges. His first two bombing runs were unsuccessful.

Hopkins recalled: "I couldn't see he dropped anything. It appeared to me he was trying to frighten the sub, and the sub just wasn't frightened."

Just behind Lingard, an R-9 Seaplane came in for a run at 500 feet. The bomb hit its mark but also did not detonate.

One Lone Submarine Brought World War I Home to the United States

The German submarine, perhaps feeling that it had achieved its mission or thinking its luck was running out, dived back below the surface and left Cape Cod.

In less than an hour, the attack was over. The Perth Amboy was still afloat, although heavily damaged, and three of the four barges were on their way to the bottom of the ocean. While no one was killed in the attack, two crew members were sent off to a Boston hospital badly injured.

Feldt and his U-156 continued attacking ships running up through Canada and Newfoundland. However, just two months before the Nov. 11 Armistice, the sub failed to clear the Northern Barrage minefield between Britain and Norway. It was never heard from again.

Lingard never got to see the Armistice, dying of pneumonia just a week before his 27th birthday—less than two weeks before the end of the war.

DEATH IN THE FINAL MINUTES OF WORLD WAR I HIGHLIGHTED FOLLY OF WAR

Saint-Symphorien, Belgium

WITH THE CLOCK TICKING DOWN to mere seconds in a four-year conflict that had already killed millions, the folly of death and destruction in World War I became ever more incomprehensible. Yet, even then it could not be stopped.

With both sides in the war already knowing for hours a ceasefire would start at 11 A.M. on the 11th day of the 11th month in 1918, hundreds of good men kept falling that morning.

Fear the other side would not abide by the conditions of the armistice, a sheer hatred produced by four years of unprecedented slaughter, blind ambition of commanders who craved that last victory, the inane joy of killing, reason enough not to let humanity shine through a few minutes, hours early. Put together they trumped the lives of soldiers, many of whom were convinced they were on the brink of peace and survival.

With two minutes to go, Canadian Private George Lawrence Price was shot by a German sniper close to Mons in southern Belgium. Another life shattered in its prime at 25.

Some 250 kilometers (150 miles) away on the Western Front in France, an American soldier, Henry Gunther, for reasons still hard to explain a century later, stormed a German post with only one minute left before the armistice and was mowed down by machine gun fire. He was 23.

"Gunther's act is seen as almost a symbol of the futility of the larger war," said U.S. historian Alec Bennett. "He was the last American. I believe he may have been the last soldier on any side to die in World War I."

Any soldier who died that morning might well be an equal symbol of futility, and the mark of "Nov. 11, 1918" on any headstone at a World War I cemetery makes it especially poignant.

"It was a matter of minutes," said Corentin Rousman, a Belgian historian working in Mons, where British empire soldiers had their first battle with the Germans in August 1914, and also their last over four years later, when Price perished.

For Commonwealth commanders it must have been especially sweet to retake the city, bringing the war to a full circle right where they lost their first soldier, English Private John Parr who had stumbled onto the Germans on Aug. 21, 1914.

In between, World War I had claimed some 14 million lives, including nine million soldiers, sailors and airmen from 28 countries. Early on, Germany came close to a quick victory before the conflict settled into hellish trench warfare. One battle, like the Somme in France could have up to a million casualties. Poison gas came to epitomize the cruel ruthlessness of a war the likes of which history had never seen.

When the old European powers were close to exhaustion in the war of attrition it came to newer nations like Gunther's United States and Price's Canada to make the difference.

Price had been a farm laborer in Saskatchewan when the swirl of history picked him off the land in 1917 as the allies sought ever more manpower to keep the Germans at bay on the Western Front.

The following summer he was part of the allied surge, and despite being gassed, he took city upon village upon city—right up to the morning of Nov. 11.

News of the impending ceasefire was already known, still he decided to go check out some homes along the historic network of industrial canals while in the center of Mons citizens already broke out the wine and whisky they had hidden for years to celebrate the liberation of their ancient medieval city.

"Then it is unclear what happens," said Rousman. Either Price runs out of a home to help someone or he thinks the war is over. What happened instead was that a shot rang out across a canal and Price dropped.

"There no longer was any massive artillery around. It really was one man, here and there, who was driven by vengeance, by a need to kill one last time," Rousman said.

And minutes not only counted for the dead but also for the killers.

"There are rules in war," Rousman said. "There is always the possibility to kill two minutes before a ceasefire. Two minutes after, the German would have had to stand before a judge. That's the difference."

The soldier who shot Price was never identified, swallowed up in a German retreat.

In senseless death, Price made the war come full circle at the level of soldiers.

With leaves falling on Saint Symphorien cemetery just outside Mons, Price, the last Commonwealth victim killed in the war, lies within a stone's throw from Parr, the first one.

"He is not forgotten," said Rousman. "It's a soldier whose tomb is often draped in flowers, notes and Canadian flags."

AP WAS THERE

THE FOLLOWING IS THE REAL-TIME reporting by The Associated Press declaring the end of World War I.

FLASH
ARMISTICE SIGNED
BULLETIN
By The Associated Press

WASHINGTON, MONDAY, NOV 11 (AP)—The Armistice between Germany, on the one hand, and the Allied governments and the United States, on the other, has been signed.

The State Department announced at 2:45 o'clock this morning that Germany had signed.

The world war will end at 6 o'clock this morning, Washington time, 11 o'clock Paris time.

Nov. 11, 1918
WAR IS OVER

WASHINGTON, NOV 11 (AP)—The greatest war in history ended Monday morning at 6 o'clock Washington time, after 1,567 days of horror, during which virtually the whole civilized world had been convulsed.

Announcement of the tremendous event was made at the State Department at the capital at 2:45 o'clock Monday morning and in a few seconds was flashed throughout the continent by the Associated Press.

The terse announcement at the State Department did not tell anything of the scene at Marshall Foch's headquarters at the time the Armistice was signed. It was stated, however, that at 6 o'clock Paris time, the signatures of Germany's delegates were fixed to the document which blasted forever the dreams which embroiled the world in a struggle which has cost, at the very lowest estimate, 10,000,000 lives.

Nov. 11, 1918
LAST BLOW OF WAR
By Atlantic Cable and AP

WITH THE AMERICAN ARMY ON THE SEDAN FRONT, NOV 11, 2PM (AP)—Thousands of American heavy guns fired the parting shot to the Germans at exactly 11 o'clock this morning.

The line reached by the American forces at 11 o'clock today was being staked out this afternoon.

The Germans hurled a few shells into Verdun just before 11 o'clock.

On the entire American front from the Moselle to the region of Sedan, there was artillery activity in the morning, all the batteries, preparing for the final salvos.

At many batteries the artillerists joined hands, forming a long line as the lanyard of the final shot. There was a few seconds of silence as the shell shot through the heavy mist. Then the gunners cheered.

American flags were raised by the soldiers over their dugouts and at the various headquarters.

Northeast of Verdun, the American infantry began to advance at 9 o'clock this morning, after artillery preparation, in the direction of the Ornes. The German artillery responded feebly, but the machine-gun resistance was stubborn. Nevertheless, the Americans made progress. The Americans had received orders to hold the positions reached by 11 o'clock, and at those positions they began to dig in, marking the advanced positions of the Americans when hostilities ceased.

Along the American front, the 11th hour was like awaiting the arrival of the New Year.

AP Was There

The gunners continued to fire, counting the shells as the time approached. The infantry were advancing, glancing at their watches. The men holding at other places organized their position to make themselves more secure.

Then the individual groups unfurled the Stars and Stripes, shook hands and cheered. Soon afterwards, they were preparing for luncheon. All the boys were hungry, as they had breakfast early in anticipation of what they expressed as the greatest day in American history.

Courtesy of the AP Corporate Archives.

AFTERWORD

IT'S THE SHATTERED LIVES AND devastation that remain with me from all the wars.

As an AP correspondent who witnessed wars in Vietnam, Afghanistan, the Mideast and Bosnia, and the genocide in Rwanda, I personally despair at seeing history repeat itself, throughout the past century, with increasingly sophisticated weapons. And I keep asking myself why hasn't the world learned anything from the death and despair that World War I and other conflicts left behind?

The Great War of 1914–1918 was supposed to be the "war to end all wars." It was not to be. It spawned revolutions, and the bitter rivalries when the fighting ended helped sow the seeds for an even bigger war two decades later.

World War II, which lasted from 1939 to 1945, involved more than 100 million people from over 30 countries around the world. Historians have called it the deadliest conflict in human history with between 50 and 85 million fatalities including from the genocide of Jews in the Holocaust, and the only use of nuclear weapons in war in Japan.

The United Nations was established on the ashes of World War II with the stated purpose "to save succeeding generations from the scourge of war." But in the more than 70 years since its creation, the U.N.—and its member states now numbering 193 countries—have failed to achieve that goal which remains a very distant dream.

It's true that there has not been a Third World War, but there have been so many others from Korea and the Arab-Israeli wars to Syria, Yemen and South Sudan.

Afterword

U.N. Secretary-General Antonio Guterres said the number of countries with violent conflicts in 2018 is the highest in the last 30 years—and low intensity conflicts since 2007 have increased by 60 percent. He lamented that the level of people killed in battle today was ten times the number in 2005.

In a globalized world united by modern technology, the U.N. chief warned world leaders that "trust is at a breaking point" and polarization and populism are increasing. He said: "World order is increasingly chaotic. Power relations are less clear. Universal values are being eroded. Democratic principles are under siege."

There is at least one certainty in this grim outlook for the world: The Associated Press will be striving to make sense of these turbulent events and to help write that very critical first draft of history with accuracy, objectivity and balance.

—Edie M. Lederer, AP Chief Correspondent at the United Nations

APPENDIX

WORLD WAR I: TIMELINE OF EVENTS

1914

June 28 — Archduke of Austria Franz Ferdinand assassinated
July 28 — Austria-Hungary declare war on Serbia
Aug 1 — Germany declares war on Russia
Aug 2 — Germany invades Luxembourg
Aug 3 — Germany declares war on France
Aug 4 — Germany declares war and invades Belgium-Schlieffen Plan
Aug 4 — Britain declares war on Germany
Aug 6 — Austria-Hungary declare war on Russia
Aug 7 — British Expeditionary Force lands in France
Aug 12 — Britain declares war on Austria-Hungary
Aug 16 — Germany army takes Liege, Belgium
Aug 16 — Battle of Cer
Aug 18 — Germany army takes Namur, Belgium
Aug 20 — Germany army takes Brussels, Belgium
Aug 20 — Battle of the Ardennes
Aug 21 — Battle of the Frontiers
Aug 23 — Battle of Mons
Aug 24 — Indian troops depart for Europe
Aug 25 — Siege of Maubeuge, France
Aug 25 — Zeppelin drops bombs on Antwerp, Belgium
Aug 25 — Japan declares war on Germany
Aug 26 — Battle of Le Cateau, France
Aug 26 — Battle of Tannenberg
Aug 31 — Germany troops enter Picardy region of France

Timeline of Events

Sept 3 — Battle of Lemberg and Battle of Masurian Lake (Eastern Front)
Sept 6 — First battle of the Marne
Sept 17 — Race to the Sea
Sept 13 — Battle of the Meuse Argonne — Battle of the Aisne
Oct 3 — Canadian Expeditionary Force leaves for Britain
Oct 5 — First aerial combat kill
Oct 6 — Fortresses of Antwerp, Belgium fall
Oct 8 — Bombing of Antwerp, Belgium
Oct 10 — Germany army takes Antwerp, Belgium
Oct 12 — Battle of La Bassee, Messines and Armentieres
Oct 16 — Indian army leaves for Mesopotamia
Oct 18 — First Battle of Ypres
Oct 29 — Turkey enters the war
Nov 10 — Fall of Diksmuide, Belgium
Nov 1 — Departure of first Anzac troops to Britain
Nov — Beginning of trench warfare
Nov 2 — Russia declares war on Turkey
Nov 2 — British launch naval blockade of Germany
Nov 5 — Britain and France declare war on Turkey
Dec 2 — Austria Hungary capture Belgrade
Dec 3 — Anzac troops diverted to Cairo
Dec 8 — Battle of the Falkland Islands
Dec 16 — German battleship bombardment of Scarborough and Hartlepool
Dec 17 — Turkey attacks Russia
Dec 18 — Battle of Givenchy
Dec 20 — First battle of Champagne
Dec 25 — Unofficial Christmas Truce

1915

Jan 19 — First Zeppelin raid on Britain
Jan 24 — Battle of Dogger Bank
Jan 31 — First use of poison gas on Eastern Front
Feb 4 — Germany in unrestricted U-boat campaign

World War I

Feb 8 — Battle of Masuria
Feb 19 — British bombardment of forts in Dardanelles Straits
March 10 — Battle of Neuve Chapelle, Western Front
March 21 — German airship raid
March 22 — Russia captures Prztmysl, Eastern Front
April 15 — Allied troops land in Gallipoli
April 18 — French pilot Roland Garros shot down and lands behind German lines
April 22 — Second Battle of Ypres — First use of chlorine gas
May 2 — Battle of Gorlice
May 7 — Lusitania sunk by German U-boat
May 9 — Kitcheners new army begins overseas deployment
May 9 — French offensive Battle of the Artois
May 9 — Battle of Aubers Ridge
May 15 — German airship raid on London
May 15 — Battle of Festubert, France
May 23 — Italy declares war on Germany and Austria
June 22 — Austria Hungary recapture Lemberg
July 9 — German forces surrender to Gen Botha, in German Southwest Africa
July 18 — Battle of Isonzo
Aug 5 — Germans take Warsaw
Aug 6 — Landing in Gallipoli
Aug 9 — Battle of Van
Aug 16 — German U-boat shells Whitehaven, Britain
Aug 25 — German, Austria, Hungary capture Brest Litovsk
Sept 25 — Battle of Loos
Sept 2 — Second Battle of Champagne
Sept 2 — Third Battle of Artois
Oct 5 — British and French land in Salonika
Oct 5 — Bulgaria enters the war
Oct 9 — Austrian forces capture Belgrade
Oct 12 — Execution of nurse Edith Cavell
Oct 14 — Bulgaria declares war on Serbia
Nov 22 — Serbian forces defeated by Germany, Austria and Hungary
Nov 22 — Battle of Ctesiphon, Mesopotamia

Timeline of Events

Dec 6 — Chantilly conference to determine Allied plans for 1916
Dec 7 — Siege of Kut, Mesopotamia
Dec 20 — Allies begin to evacuate Gallipoli

1916

Jan 9 — Allies withdraw from Gallipoli completed
Jan 24 — Conscription introduced in Britain
Feb 18 — German forces in Cameroons surrender to British
Feb 21 — Battle of Verdun
March 9 — Germany declares war on Portugal
April 29 — British forces surrender to Turkish in Kut
May 14 — Battle of Asiago, Italian Front
May 31 — Battle of Jutland
June 4 — Brusilov Offensive
June 5 — HMS Hampshire sunk, Lord Kitchener drowns
July 1 — Battle of the Somme
July 14 — Battle of Delville Wood
July 14 — Battle of Bazentin Ridge
July 19 — Battle of Fromelles
Aug 6 — Battle of the Isonzo
Aug 27 — Romania enters war and is invaded by Germany
Aug 28 — Italy declares war on Germany
Sept 3 — First German airship shot down over Britain
Sept 4 — British take Dar es Salaam in German East Africa
Sept 15 — First use of tanks en masse on the Somme
Sept 17 — Red Baron wins first aerial combat kill in Cambrai
Oct 5 — Soldier Adolf Hitler wounded
Oct 24 — Nivelle offensive in Verdun
Nov 13 — Battle of the Ancre
Dec 6 — Central Powers capture Bucharest
Dec 9 — Romania signs Armistice with Central Powers
Dec 19 — End of the Battle of Verdun
Dec 23 — Battle of Magdhaba — Allied forces defeat Turkish in Sinai Peninsula

1917

Jan 9 — Battle of Rafa
March — Bagdad falls to Anglo-Indian
March — German begin a retreat to the Hindenburg Line
April 6 — America declares war on Germany
April 9 — Battle of Arras
April — Battle for Vimy Ridge
April 16 — Failed French offensive at Chemin des Dames
April — Battle at Beaumont Hamel
April — Battle of Bullecourt
May 18 — Selective Service act passed in US
June — Deadliest German air raid on London
July 1 — Kerensky offensive
July 31 — Battle of Passchendaele
Aug — Battle of Hill 70 in France
Aug 6 — Battle of Marasesti
Sept 26 — Battle of Polygon Wood
Oct 15 — Mata Hari executed
Oct 24 — Battle of Caporetto
Oct 31 — Battle of Beersheba
Oct 26 — Brazil declares war with Central Powers
Nov 6 — British offensive on Western Front
Nov 20 — British tank victory at Cambrai
Dec 5 — Armistice signed by Russia and Germany
Dec 7 — United States declares war on Austria
Dec 9 — Battle of Jerusalem

1918

Jan 8 — Fourteen Points Plan layed out by US President Wilson
March 3 — Treaty of Brest Litovsk signed by Russia and Germany
March 21 — Battle of Picardy
March 30 — Battle of Villers-Bretonneaux
April 9 — German spring offensive in Flanders
April 21 — Red Baron shot down and killed near Amiens

Timeline of Events

May — German attack on Chemin des Dames
May 28 — Battle of Cantigny
June 1 — Battle of Belleau Wood
June 15 — Battle of the Piave River
July 21 — German U-boat fires on Cape Cod, USA, only attack on mainland America
July 15 — German offensive at Champagne
July 18 — Battle of Chateau Thierry
July 18 — Second Battle of the Marne
Aug 8 — Hundred Days Offensive launched by the Allies
Aug 21 — Third Battle of the Somme
Sept 12 — Battle of St. Mihiel
Sept 19 — Turkish forces collapse at Megiddo
Sept 26 — Battle of the Meuse Argonne
Sept 28 — Final offensive at Houthulst Forest
Oct 4 — Germany asks for Armistice
Oct 24 — Battle of Vittorio Veneto
Oct 29 — German Navy mutiny
Oct 30 — Turkey makes peace signs Armistice of Mudros
Oct 31 — Dissolution of Austro-Hungarian empire
Nov 3 — Armistice of Villa Giusti to end war with Italy and Austro-Hungarians
Nov 9 — Germany's Kaiser Wilhelm II abdicates
Nov 11 — Germany signs armistice ending the war

WORLD WAR I:
PHOTO TIMELINE

The Archduke of Austria Franz Ferdinand, center right, and his wife Sophie, center left, walk to their car in Sarajevo. This photo was taken on June 28, 1914 minutes before the assassination of the Archduke and his wife, an event which set off a chain reaction of events which would eventually lead to World War One.

Police pursue a suspect after the shooting of Austria's Archduke Franz Ferdinand in Sarajevo, Yugoslavia on June 28, 1914. Young Serb nationalist Gavrilo Princip fired the shots that assassinated the Archduke and his wife.

Russian reservists walk with their belongings in St. Petersburg, Russia, August 8, 1914. Russia entered World War One with an army which was massive but badly armed.

Prussian soldiers leaving Berlin for the front are given flowers by a woman during World War One. (Undated)

World War One Belgian troops set out from Brussels in the direction of Louvain. (Undated)

Damage to one of the forts at Liege, Belgium, circa 1914. On August 5th that same year, the Battle of Liege began, the siege lasted longer than planned and may have delayed the German advance into France.

Serbian soldiers take position on the battle line. Some of the first battles of World War One were fought between Serbia and Austria-Hungary around the Cer Mountain region. (Undated)

German army troops receive rations from a field transport while advancing toward Brussels. In mid-August 1914 the German army launched its assault on Brussels.

German troops stand in formation during the occupation of Brussels in August 1914.

A bridge across the Meuse River in Belgium, which was destroyed by retreating Belgian troops, is being rebuilt by invading German troops, circa 1914.

A Belgian machine gun detachment sets up near Haelen, Belgium, August 1914. The Belgians often used dogs to draw the ammunitions cart. The Battle of Haelen was also known as the Battle of the Silver Helmets.

A man stands next to a building damaged by shrapnel from bombs dropped from a Zeppelin in Antwerp, Belgium, circa 1914. Antwerp was damaged heavily during World War One.

The Cathedral of Reims in France smokes after bombardment during World War One during September 1914. The advancing German Army heavily damaged the city.

Indian troops arrive in France during World War One. (Undated)

German soldiers speak with each other on the Western Front during World War One. (Undated)

France's battle torn Marne district is reduced to rubble and mud during World War One. (Undated)

German troops march through the streets of Antwerp, Belgium during World War One, circa 1914.

People crowd the Antwerp quaysides as they prepare for an exodus out of the city during World War One, circa 1914.

Belgian civilians and a cavalry detail move out of the pathway of the German advance during World War One in Antwerp, Belgium, October 14, 1914.

Small boats, pushed together, create a pontoon bridge over the Scheldt River in Antwerp, Belgium circa 1914. The bridge was constructed during World War One for residents and troops to escape the German Army.

Allied troops huddle in a trench around a tiny fire near Ypres, Belgium, circa 1914.

Damage from German bombardment to the lighthouse in Scarborough, England during World War One, December 1914.

Damage to the Royal Hotel in Scarborough, England after a bombing raid, December 1914.

Bodies on a battlefield after the battle of Champagne in France during World War One. (Undated)

Serbian troops on the promenade of the public gardens in Belgrade. (Undated)

German soldiers gather at Christmas at an unknown location during World War One, circa 1914.

A lone wounded Austrian soldier lies on the field of battle during World War One. (Undated)

Allied soldiers eat and drink in a shell hole in France during World War One. (Undated)

Soldiers of the French Red Cross transport a wounded soldier to a first aid station immediately after the battle of Flanders in Belgium. (Undated)

Australian troops arrive in Alexandria, Egypt, en route to the battlefield on the Gallipoli Peninsula during World War One, circa 1915.

A Turkish soldier takes aim at British troops, while another watches carefully, from a trench in Gallipoli, Turkey, circa 1915.

A Turkish cannon moves to the front lines on the Gallipoli Peninsula, Turkey, during World War One. (Undated)

Mustafa Kemal Ataturk, military Commander of the Turkish troops in Gallipoli, Turkey, looks over the battlefield during World War One, circa 1915.

French troops man a lookout in France during a battle in the Argonne Forest during World War One. (Undated)

German troops cut a barbed wire fence in an unknown location. (Undated)

A bridge, an abandoned tank and shell craters full of water on the battlefield in St. Julien, Belgium, circa 1915.

An unidentified soldier, wearing a gas mask around his neck, bangs on a frying pan as a gas warning on the field near Reims, France. (Undated)

Turkish soldiers form a queue to get water from a fountain, behind their lines in Gallipoli, Turkey, circa 1915.

Turkish soldiers take a rest during fighting, with their guns in their hands, in a trench in Gallipoli, Turkey, circa 1915.

The British cargo and passenger ship Lusitania as it set out for England on its last voyage from New York City, May 1, 1915. The British ocean liner was sunk off Ireland on May 7th by a German U-Boat, killing 1,150 people, 114 of them Americans.

The U Boat 139, which sank the Lusitania in an unknown location. The British liner was sank on May 7, 1915, by a German submarine off the southern coast of Ireland. Among those who perished were Charles Frohman, Alfred G. Vanderbilt and Elbert Hubbard.

Troops are mobilized on the bank of the Danube River across from Belgrade during World War One (Date Unknown). Austrian forces captured the Serbian capitol on October 9, 1915.

Turkish soldiers raise their flag at Kanli Sirt, Gallipoli, Turkey during World War One, circa 1915.

A British recruiting poster displays Field Marshal Herbert Kitchener in 1914. The poster reads "Your Country Needs You." Kitchener's Army was a group of all-volunteer soldiers formed in the United Kingdom.

French soldiers move troops and cargo at Nixeville, France, during the World War One Battle of Verdun, April 8, 1916.

One of the batteries of the famous French 75's at Douaumont, France during the World War One Battle of Verdun. (Undated)

Gen. Sir Sam Hughes and an unidentified group look at ruins in Arras, France during World War One, August 1916.

French troops attend to the funeral of an unknown aviator at an unknown location, circa 1916.

Turkish soldiers at a military review at Damascus, Syria. (Undated)

The German fleet with battle cruisers on the way in the North Sea to meet the British Grand Fleet in the Battle of Jutland during World War One, May 31, 1916.

German troops man a machine gun post from a trench at the Vistula River in Russia during World War One, circa 1916.

The British Grand Fleet under admiral John Jellicoe on their way to meet the Imperial German Navy's fleet for the Battle of Jutland in the North Sea, May 31, 1916.

Australian artillery soldiers operate a large caliber gun at the Somme front, in France during World War One, circa 1916.

French soldiers carry the wounded during the World War One Battle of the Somme, France. (Undated)

French Captain Georges Guynemer in front of his shot-down plane in Piennes, France during World War One, September 24, 1916.

Soldiers attend a burial in back of the battle lines in Pervyse, Belgium. (Undated)

French troops walk on regained ground near the River Meuse, near Beaumont, France during World War One, August 1917.

French troops in a shell hole during the offensive which resulted in its winning back of the Chemin des Dames in France at the end of October 1917.

The battlefield, pockmarked with craters filled with water, after the major World War One Battle of Verdun, France, circa 1917.

President Woodrow Wilson delivers a speech to the joint session of Congress, in Washington, United States, during World War One, April 2, 1917.

German soldiers bring in Canadian wounded during the Battle of Vimy, France during World War One, circa 1917.

German mine-throwing troops, at an attack at the Keil and Poehl mounts, Germany. (Undated)

World War One Canadian soldiers carry a stretcher through the mud near Boesinghe, Belgium, circa 1917.

A Canadian soldier helps an injured German soldier to a dressing station. (Undated)

An unidentified World War One soldier walks along wooden planks placed over the mud of Flanders' Fields near the Yperlee Canal near Ypres, Belgium, circa 1917.

British World War One soldiers return in formation to Ypres, Belgium, circa 1917.

The cathedral in the town square of Ypres, Belgium, is in ruins after bombing in World War One. (Undated)

Wounded Canadian and German World War One soldiers help one another through the mud during the Battle of Passchendaele in Passchendaele, Belgium, circa 1917.

World War One wounded are being placed in ambulance during the advance on Lens, France. (Undated)

Dancer "Mata Hari", who was born Margaretha Geertruida Zelle poses in an unknown location. Zelle was executed October 15, 1917 during World War One for spying for Germany.

An old type tank from World War One, circa 1917. Tanks came into use during World War One and increased the mobility of soldiers who were mainly fighting a trench war. Their design was taken from farm vehicles.

British troops run under heavy fire outside Cambrai, France during World War One. (Undated)

A World War One trench winds through the village of Brabant-en-Meuse near Verdun, France in 1917.

Smoke billows out of buildings in Cambrai, France, after being bombarded by German forces during the World War One Battle of Cambrai, December 1917.

British General Sir Edmund Allenby enters the captured city of Jerusalem, during World War One, December 9, 1917.

Wounded World War One soldiers play a game at a London hospital. (Undated)

Members of the first contingent of New Yorkers drafted into the United States Army line up in front of their barracks at Camp Upton, Yaphank, Long Island, N.Y., circa 1917.

The first troops of the American Expeditionary Force land at the French port of St. Nazaire, France, June 1917.

The first 5,000 American soldiers to reach England march across historic Westminster Bridge in London, circa 1917. (AP Photo/U.S. Army Signal Corps)

U.S. Army General John J. Pershing, center, inspects French troops at Boulogne, France, June 13, 1917.

An American soldier from the First Division throws a hand grenade in battle during World War One along the Western Front in France, March 15, 1918.

American soldiers of Company K, 165th Infantry of the Fighting 69th, Old Rainbow Division, march to the trenches at St. Clement, France during World War One, March 1918.

A field of barbed wire in a no-man's land near Ancerviller, France, during World War One, April 25, 1918. The area was a sector of the 2nd Battalion, 165th Infantry. (AP Photo/U.S. Army Signal Corps)

German flying ace Manfred von Richthofen, also known as the "Red Baron," is shown returning from a mission at his squadron's aerodrome, circa 1916. Von Richthofen was shot down and killed over France in April 1918.

Two soldiers are passed by tanks on their way to support French troops in Juvigny, France, during World War One. (Undated)

The 28th Infantry Regiment of the First Division, A.E.F. goes over the top of a trench during an American offensive of World War One in the Battle of Cantigny, France, May 28, 1918.

Soldiers attend the burial of fellow soldiers and two Canadian nurses, killed in German air raid, during World War One. (Undated)

United States Army troops stand in the trenches in France during World War One. (Undated)

American troops carrying guns with fixed bayonets climb over a sandbag revetment in France during World War One, circa 1918.

Italian army soldiers look out of their dugouts at the Battle of the Piave River, Italy during World War One. The Battle of the Piave River was fought June 15 through June 23, 1918.

Members of the Red Cross sort the backpacks of dead and wounded soldiers in France, during World War One, circa 1918.

American troops from the 18th Infantry, First Division, pause in a ruined French town near St. Mihiel, France during World War One, July 1918.

U.S. troops of the 107th Regiment Infantry, 27th Division, advance on a path through a barbed wire entanglement near Beauqueanes, Somme, France during World War One, September 13, 1918. (AP Photo/U.S. Army Signal Corps)

German reserves being rushed to front by trucks in Germany. (Undated)

U.S. Marines respond to a gas attack near Verdun, France during World War One, circa 1918.

A U.S. Army 37-mm gun crew man their position during the World War One Meuse-Argonne Allied offensive in France, September 26, 1918.

American soldiers from New York, who served on the frontline in Cambria, France, rig up a Liberty Bell to celebrate the signing of the Armistice to end World War One, November 1918.

A group of people gather in front of Buckingham Palace in London, England to celebrate the signing of the Armistice that ended the fighting of World War One, November 11, 1918.

People in the streets of Paris, France, celebrate the signing of the Armistice that ended the fighting of World War One, November 11, 1918.

American troops, near St. Mihiel, France, cheer after hearing the news that the Armistice has been signed, ending World War One, circa 1918.

ABOUT THE EDITORS

Raf Casert has covered the European Union and other international institutions in Brussels and across the continent on top of international sporting events like the Olympics and the World Cup around the globe during a 34-year career at the Associated Press. He is currently Benelux News Editor.

Virginia Mayo has covered the European Union and NATO both in Brussels and beyond as well as other international events such as the G8, G20, Cannes Film Festival and World Economic Forum during her 18 years with the Associated Press. She is graduate of Emerson College in Boston, MA.

ABOUT THE CONTRIBUTORS

Robert H. Reid has had a lifelong interest in military history. He served for three years in the US Army in Germany during the Cold War. He spent nearly 35 years as an Associated Press foreign correspondent, covering revolutions and armed conflicts in such places as Iran, Afghanistan, Poland, Bosnia, Lebanon, Libya, Sudan, Cambodia, the Philippines, Kosovo and Egypt during the Arab Spring.

Edith M. Lederer has worked on every continent except Antarctica during a 52-year career with The Associated Press. The first woman assigned full-time to the AP staff reporting the Vietnam War, Lederer was also AP's first female bureau chief overseas, based in Lima, Peru. In addition to wars, she helped cover the downfall of communism, the break-up of the Soviet Union and the Romanian revolution. She has been AP's chief correspondent at the United Nations since 1998 and has written about the diplomatic side of conflicts and major global issues from the nuclear programs in Iran and North Korea to climate change, combating poverty and women's rights.

BYLINES

THE TRAGEDY OF WORLD WAR I IN ONE SOLDIER'S STORY
By Raf Casert
Contributors: Virginia Mayo, Martin Benedyk, Robert Reid
Photo by Virginia Mayo

SARAJEVO: THE POLITICAL SLAYING THAT SET OFF
WORLD WAR I
By Aida Cerkez
Photo by Charlie Riedel

BLIND TO TRAGEDY, EUROPE STARTED WORLD WAR I
By Raf Casert
Photo by Virginia Mayo

WORLD WAR I TRENCHES IN ENGLAND HIGHLIGHT TRAINING FOR
THE REAL HORRORS OF WAR
By Jill Lawless
Photo by Lefteris Pitarakis

TOUR DE FRANCE, TOO, WAS STEEPED IN WORLD WAR I HORRORS
By Greg Keller
Photo by Christophe Ena

BEFORE 'SAVING PRIVATE RYAN,' PVT. SMITH WAS SAVED
By Danica Kirka
Photo by Scott Heppell

Bylines

WORLD WAR I SPREAD FLOWERS AROUND TOO,
AND NOT ONLY POPPIES
By Chad Garland
Photo by Rick Bowmer

CULTURAL HERITAGE SO OFTEN ONE OF FIRST VICTIMS
OF WAR
By Raf Casert
Contributors: Virginia Mayo, Mark Carlson
Photo by Virginia Mayo

WORLD WAR I AVIATION STILL ALIVE, AND SWOOPING,
AT AERODROME IN NEW YORK
By Michael Hill
Photo by Mike Groll

WORLD WAR I: THE HORRORS OF WAR THAT INSPIRED
INNOVATIVE ART
By Hillel Italie
Photo by Virginia Mayo

THE DAY FRANCE RELIED ON ITS CABBIES TO BOOST
ITS WAR EFFORT
By Jamie Keaton
Contributor: Raf Casert
Photo by Thibault Camus

THEY NEVER WILTED. POPPIES LIVE ON AS ENDURING
SYMBOL OF THE WAR
By Sylvia Hui
Photo by Virginia Mayo

IN 1914 AMID THE GREAT WAR, THE GREATEST OF
CHAMPAGNE VINTAGES
By Raf Casert
Contributor: Virginia Mayo
Photo by Virginia Mayo

World War I

A CENTURY LATER, BRITISH ARMY HONORS SOLDIERS KILLED IN WWI
By Greg Keller
Photo by Virginia Mayo

CHRISTMAS 1914: THE DAY EVEN WORLD WAR I SHOWED HUMANITY
By Raf Casert
Contributor: Virginia Mayo
Photo by Virginia Mayo

A LANDSCAPE SHAPED BY WAR
By Virginia Mayo
Photo by Virginia Mayo

A CENTURY LATER, A MYTHIC THUD OF A FOOTBALL IN WARTIME IS STILL HEARD
By Raf Casert
Contributor: Virginia Mayo
Photo by Virginia Mayo

FIRST GAS ATTACKS UNLEASHED NEW HORRORS AND CHANGED WARFARE
By Raf Casert
Contributor: Virginia Mayo
Photo by Virginia Mayo

VICTOR IN THE BOSTON MARATHON ONE YEAR, A VICTIM OF WORLD WAR I THE NEXT
By Raf Casert
Contributor: Virginia Mayo
Photo by Virginia Mayo

MEMORIES STILL HAUNT BOTH SIDES OF THE GALLIPOLI TRAGEDY
By Desmond Butler
Photo by Lefteris Pitarakis

ALAN SEEGER, POET-SOLDIER, WHO FOUGHT AS AN AMERICAN WITH FRANCE IN WORLD WAR I
By Raf Casert
Contributors: Virginia Mayo, Mark Carlson
Photo by Virginia Mayo

Bylines

THE UNITED STATES JOINED WORLD WAR I
TO MAKE THE DIFFERENCE
By Raf Casert and Virginia Mayo
Photo by Virginia Mayo

INNOVATIONS A CENTURY AGO, BUT STILL WITH US
By Chris Carola

VIMY—THE WORLD WAR I BATTLE THAT DEFINED CANADA
By Raf Casert and Rob Gillies
Contributors: Dave Rising, Sylvie Corbet
Photo by Virginia Mayo

SPY, TEMPTRESS, VICTIM? MATA HARI STILL
ELUDES DEFINITION
By Raf Casert
Photo by Virginia Mayo

ONE VICTOROUS BATTLE THAT BECAME
A DEFINING MOMENT FOR THE UNITED STATES
By Raf Casert
Contributors: Virginia Mayo, Mark Carlson
Photo by Virginia Mayo

WORLD WAR I MUNITIONS STILL MAKING THEIR WAY
ONTO THE BEACHES AN OCEAN AWAY
By Wayne Parry
Photo by Mel Evans

ONE LONE SUBMARINE BROUGHT WORLD WAR I HOME
TO THE UNITED STATES
By Virginia Mayo and Raf Casert
Photo by Virginia Mayo

DEATH IN THE FINAL MINUTES OF WWI HIGHLIGHTED
FOLLY OF WAR
By Raf Casert
Contributor: Virginia Mayo

ACKNOWLEDGMENTS

THE EDITORS WOULD LIKE TO THANK the following for their contributions: American Battle Monuments Commission, British Ministry of Defense, Commonwealth War Graves Commission, DOVO Dienst voor opruiming en vernietiging van ontploffingstuigen, Flemish Heritage Institute, Fries Museum, German War Graves Commission, Imperial War Museum, In Flanders Fields Museum, Last Post Association, Museum of the Great War, Memorial Museum Passchendaele 1917, Orleans Historical Society, Western Front Association, Kaylene Biggs, Hubert de Billy, Ann Callens, Helene Chaulin, Piet Chielens, U.S. Army Col. David S. Jones, Maureen Kiesewetter, Marie Legrand, Patrick Lernhout, Sandy Logan, Margaret MacMillan, John H. Morrow Jr., Lourens Oldersma, Marcel Queyrat, Pierre-Emmanuel Taittinger, Mary Thompson, Reine Van Cutsem and Julie Wheelwright

THE ASSOCIATED PRESS WOULD LIKE TO THANK Raf Casert, Virginia Mayo, Robert H. Reid, Martin Benedyk, Rick Bowmer, Desmond Butler, Thibault Camus, Mark Carlson, Chris Carola, Aida Cerkez, Sylvie Corbet, Matt Dunham, Christophe Ena, Mel Evans, Chad Garland, Rob Gillies, Mike Groll, Scott Heppell, Michael Hill, Sylvia Hui, Hillel Italie, Jamey Keaten, Greg Keller, Danica Kirka, Jill Lawless, Martin Meissner, Francois Mori, Wayne Parry, Lefteris Pitarakis, Laurent Rebours, Charlie Riedel, Dave Rising, Orlin Wagner, Kirsty Wigglesworth; Angela Charlton, Peter Costanzo, Valerie Komor, Mike Bowser, Chuck Zoeller, Lauren Easton, Niko Price, Trenton Daniel, Tony Hicks, Eric Carvin and Kevin Callahan.

ALSO AVAILABLE FROM AP BOOKS

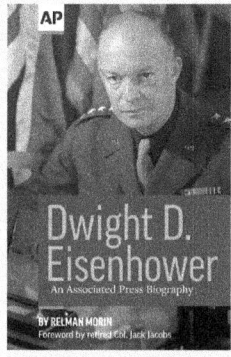

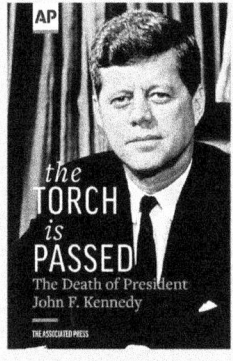

ap.org/books

www.ingramcontent.com/pod-product-compliance
Lightning Source LLC
Chambersburg PA
CBHW061645040426
42446CB00010B/1588